The Asbury Outpouring of 2023 was remarkable by most metrics—cultural, spiritual, and demographic. And the outpouring continues to be significant as its values self-seed into hundreds of locations around the world wherever people are hungry for a simpler, truer encounter with the living God. In this short record, we find the facts and the essential DNA. Our prayer is that *Taken by Surprise* will inspire and equip many more to seek God with all their hearts.

—Pete Greig
senior pastor of Emmaus Road Church, Guilford, England, and
co-founder of 24-7 Prayer International, and
author of *Red Moon Rising: Rediscover the Power of Prayer*

Simply and beautifully told, this account of the Asbury Outpouring whets the appetite for more of God and how he wants to encounter this generation of students gathered in the universities of the world and scattered across all nations.

—Rich Wilson
Fusion Movement Leader

Mark Elliott, a well-trained historian with a thorough knowledge of Asbury University's record of earlier awakenings, is perfectly positioned to offer this balanced, superbly researched, insightful, but still probing account of the much-publicized revival that took place at Asbury in February 2023. The book is particularly illuminating as it balances descriptions of the fresh wind of the Spirit (prayer, repentance, singing, reconciliation, renewal) with the event's mechanics (how many came, where from, actions by Asbury administrators, feeding the crowds, security, publicity on social media, ethnic involvement, multidenominational participation).

—Mark Noll, PhD
author of *A History of Christianity in the United States and Canada* and
America's Book: The Rise and Decline of a Bible Civilization, 1794–1911

Reading this book is like walking on the Asbury University campus and experiencing the kingdom of God: students praying and praising, repenting and reconciling; people from all over the world standing in line hungry for God; humble, invisible leaders who navigate the sudden arrival of thousands of visitors; and generous volunteers who share homes, hot dogs, water, and more. All these inspire surrender to God and multiply this experience at home. Revive us, o Lord!

—Rev. Eduard Khegay
resident bishop of the Eurasia Episcopal Area of the United Methodist Church

Mark Elliott's prolific—and invariably insightful and deeply informed—writing always inspires me. Certainly again true with *Taken by Surprise*. It is a spiritually powerful and scholarly analysis of revival at Asbury College and University from 1905 to 2023. Dr. Elliott is also known for his study of spiritual revival in the former Soviet Union and, over many years to the present, has been deeply involved in ministries there. Reading *Taken by Surprise* has left me praying and singing: "a great revival send. Begin the work with me."

—Anita Deyneka
president emeritus of Mission Eurasia and a board member of
A Family for Every Orphan

My heart was stirred as I read *Taken by Surprise*. The 2023 Asbury Spiritual Outpouring is the first campus revival during the social media age. Consequently, not only information but disinformation was broadcast far and wide. Dr. Mark Elliott has utilized social media posts and personal interviews to capture an accurate picture of what took place. I commend this well-researched and wonderfully written book. May God use it greatly to continue to kindle the flame of revival.

—**Timothy K. Beougher**, PhD
Billy Graham Professor of Evangelism and Church Growth
The Southern Baptist Theological Seminary and
author of *Invitation to Evangelism: Sharing the Gospel with Compassion and Conviction*

The Asbury Outpouring marked me forever. We have been praying for something like this for years here in Europe, and when we heard what God was doing at Asbury, we could not help ourselves but to get on a plane and fly across the Atlantic to experience it for ourselves. This fascinating book not only takes my soul back to Hughes Auditorium and what God was doing there, but also stirred in my heart to continue to cry out for springs of living water to flow in Europe and beyond.

—**Sarah Breuel**
director of Revive Europe and
evangelism training coordinator for the
International Fellowship of Evangelical Students Europe

Mark Elliott provides a masterful summary of the contexts, events, and outcomes of one of the most unique awakening movements of spiritual renewal I have encountered in five decades of ministry. Combining a thorough historical theology of revivals with a detailed but winsome and inspirational accounting of the Asbury Outpouring, I was informed, inspired, convicted, and challenged to seek greater depths of spiritual understanding and holy living.

—**David J. Gyertson**, PhD
former president of Regent, Asbury, and Taylor Universities

This essential and moving account of the 2023 Asbury Revival is notable for several reasons. Full of firsthand eyewitness reports, yet it resonates with the long course of church history. Its author is both a sympathetic insider and a critical historian. Here the special uniqueness of the Asbury Outpouring is cross-referenced to previous times of spiritual awakening both at Asbury and elsewhere. Whatever the long-term fruit of the 2023 revival may be, this on-the-spot account will provide understanding and inspiration.

—**Howard A. Snyder**, PhD
author of *The Radical Wesley and Patterns for Church Renewal*
and *Signs of the Spirit: How God Reshapes the Church*

In a superb example of emic (insider) and etic (outsider) research, Elliott synthesizes both a sympathetic reading of revivalism and a scholarly sensitivity to social dynamics. This first historical draft of a remarkable spiritual event helped make my own academic institution intelligible to me.

—**David R. Swartz**, PhD
author of *Facing West: American Evangelicals in an Age of World Christianity*
and *Moral Minority: The Evangelical Left in an Age of Conservatism*

Even those of us who are not part of a revivalist tradition can find our hearts strangely warmed by this account of the recent revival at Asbury. Mark Elliott is both a careful student of the human condition and a Holiness Wesleyan, so he is well-equipped to give a full and rich account of these events and the critical moment in our land that prompts these young people to cry out to the Lord. We are not even close to knowing God's full scope of action in our time, but this careful account provides some important connections.

—**Joel A. Carpenter**, PhD
author of *Revive Us Again: The Reawakening of American Fundamentalism*
and *Christianity Remade: The Rise of Indian-Initiated Churches*

What a blessing *Taken by Surprise* was to me, and I am sure will be for many others. In reading, there were times I was brought to tears. As a historian and scholar, Dr. Elliott appreciates the value of contemporaneous, firsthand accounts of historic events. Here he has captured many participants' life-changing encounters with God as the result of an unplanned, unique visitation of the Holy Spirit on Asbury University's campus. This is an excellent job of telling the story—facts, emotions, and passion. May the Lord use this account to continue the impact of the Holy Spirit's work among Asbury's students and so many others in February 2023.

—**Larry D. Brown**
retired partner of PricewaterhouseCoopers LLP
and chair of the Asbury University Board of Trustees

Taken by Surprise is a means of grace. Mark Elliott presents us with a sensitive, yet thorough narrative of the 2023 spontaneous Asbury Awakening. As a skilled historian, Elliott helps us see the complex, practical, miracle workings of the Holy Spirit upfront and visible, yet in holy ways of surrender and service behind. I pray this book will be more than a celebration of the revival, but most importantly, a means of grace for more great awakenings. Glory to God!

—**Jonathan S. Raymond**, PhD
president emeritus of Trinity Western University
and author of *Higher Higher Education: Integrating Holiness into All of Campus Life*

What happened on February 8, 2023, and the fifteen days following at Asbury University was historic and holy. As a member of the ministry and leadership team, I had a front-row seat to the movement of the Holy Spirit and the spontaneous work of God in the hearts of, first, our students and then the world. Dr. Mark ("Skip") Elliott chronicles the experiences of those who saw with their own eyes and heard with their own ears what God began in Hughes Auditorium that extends even now around the world. As a seasoned researcher and author, he covers the facts of the Asbury Outpouring both on the platform and behind the scenes. A huge debt of gratitude is owed to Dr. Elliott for documenting the story of how God moved! Come, Holy Spirit! Amen and amen.

—**Rev. Sarah Thomas Baldwin**, PhD
Asbury University Vice President of Student Life

taken by
surprise

taken by surprise

THE ASBURY REVIVAL OF 2023

MARK R. ELLIOTT

**Foreword by Robert E. Coleman
and Stephen A. Seamands**

Seedbed

Printed in the United States of America

Page design and layout by PerfecType, Nashville, Tennessee

Elliott, Mark R., 1947-
  Taken by Surprise : the Asbury Revival of 2023 / Mark R. Elliott ; foreword by Robert E. Coleman and Stephen A. Seamands – Franklin, Tennessee : Seedbed Publishing, ©2023.

pages ; cm.

          ISBN: 9798888000144 (paperback)
          ISBN: 9798888000151 (epub)
          ISBN: 9798888000168 (pdf)
          OCLC: 1393280936

          1. Revivals--Kentucky--Wilmore. 2. Asbury University--History. 3. Wilmore
          (Ky.)--Church history--21st century.   I. Title. II. Coleman, Robert E., 1928-
          III. Seamands, Stephen A., 1949-

BV3775.W5 E44 2023   269.209769   2023944611

SEEDBED PUBLISHING
Franklin, Tennessee
seedbed.com

To all who found release, peace, and saving grace freely bestowed by Father, Son, and Holy Spirit those February days and nights;

To all who were cleansed, refreshed, and renewed by the power and comfort of the Holy Spirit for kingdom service those sixteen days and nights; and

To all those who may yet find the consolation and joy unspeakable found in Christ Jesus:

One need not be at Asbury, and one need not be in February to pray: "Savior, do not pass me by."

contents

foreword

In 1995, I (Stephen Seamands) was supervising a student at Asbury Theological Seminary who was writing a doctoral dissertation on the Asbury Revival of 1970. As part of his research, he surveyed 237 students who had been present during the revival. Though twenty-five years had passed, so many still had graphic, vivid memories of the revival, the most common by far centering around a profound sense of the manifest presence of God. It was as if those who were there experienced a foretaste of heaven. The Lord was with us, reigning among his people in a way that could not be missed. I was a senior at Asbury College during the 1970 Revival, and that was my experience too.

I (Robert Coleman) was a seminary professor at Asbury Theological Seminary at the time. *One Divine Moment*, the book that I edited about the 1970 Asbury Revival which was published later that same year, also underscored that profound sense of God's deep, unmistakable abiding. The title was drawn from a statement of Dennis Kinlaw, president of Asbury College at the time: "Give me one divine moment when God acts, and I say that moment is far superior to all the human efforts of man throughout the centuries."

What we experienced of the presence of God in our midst during the 1970 Asbury Revival was similar to what has happened in all true revivals. Renowned Puritan scholar Richard Owen Roberts summed it up well: "Without doubt, the greatest single aspect of every true revival is the . . . mighty sense of the presence of God which draws large crowds, produces intense conviction, causes tears to flow, enables hardened sinners to right the wrongs of years past, produces seemingly instantaneous conversions, and results in spontaneous joy and enthusiasm."[1]

Now, based on extensive research and numerous firsthand interviews and reports, Mark Elliott has carefully unfolded another "divine moment" through the Asbury Outpouring of February 2023. Everything that Roberts mentioned—and more—happened in our midst: the palpable, unmistakable sense of God's presence, and perhaps most of all, the extended times of worship and praise. Many who were there had never experienced singing as sublime and heavenly. (See appendix C for the worship music of the outpouring.) Though a number of us living in Wilmore had been praying for another Asbury revival, especially during the past few years, when it happened, we were all truly "taken by surprise."

Although revivals are truly divine in so many ways, they are also profoundly human events. Through Dr. Elliott's interviews with so many who were directly involved in overseeing and shepherding the outpouring, we learn of many decisions that had to be made on the fly. Security and safety protocols had to be put in place. Intrusive persons had to be dealt with. Hundreds of volunteers had to be deployed. Altar prayer ministers had to be trained and equipped. Worship teams had to be chosen and consecrated. Those in leadership had to cope with media, especially social media (Facebook, YouTube, Instagram, TikTok). Then, as thousands of people descended upon Wilmore, other challenges arose—from parking to restrooms—that nearly overwhelmed the city and its residents.

Through Dr. Elliott's extensive interviews, conducted within three months of the outpouring with many who were at the epicenter of those extraordinary sixteen days, we learn of the amazing human backstory which was crucial in undergirding and sustaining the divine main story being played out publicly in Hughes Auditorium. *Taken by Surprise* underscores that it is a mistake to set the two aspects of the outpouring—divine and human—against each other. The same Holy Spirit who was working so palpably and powerfully in Hughes Auditorium and in the other overflow worship venues in Wilmore was also working behind the scenes. The Spirit that enabled leaders to shepherd and steward the outpouring also empowered volunteers to sustain and enhance the deep work of salvation and sanctification in our midst. The human side of the Asbury Outpouring was also divinely inspired and directed.

Both of us are longtime residents of Wilmore, and have personally experienced significant revivals at Asbury in the past (Robert Coleman in 1950 and 1970; Stephen Seamands in 1970). We are profoundly grateful and stand in awe that God has chosen to visit us once again. We wish to echo the words of the psalmist: "The LORD has done great things for us, and we are filled with joy" (Ps. 126:3). Our prayer is that readers of this informative, inspiring account of the 2023 Asbury Outpouring will be encouraged and strengthened in their faith. Above all, we ask of God, "Will you not revive us again, that your people may rejoice in you? Show us your unfailing love, LORD, and grant us your salvation" (Ps. 85:6–7).

Robert E. Coleman, PhD, is the author of *The Master Plan of Evangelism* (1963) and editor of *One Divine Moment: The Asbury Story* (1970).

Stephen A. Seamands, PhD, is the author of *Ministry in the Image of God: The Trinitarian Shape of Christian Service* (2005) and *Follow the Healer: Biblical and Theological Foundations for Healing Ministry* (2023).

preface

GETTING PERSONAL

Wednesday, February 8, 2023, my wife and I left Wilmore, Kentucky, at 5:00 a.m. on our way to Florida. We were on Interstate 75 somewhere near the Tennessee-Georgia line by the time a regularly scheduled chapel service got underway on the campus of Asbury University in Wilmore. By the time we found a motel in Gainesville, Florida, after a long day's drive, hundreds of students were singing and praying in Hughes Auditorium of their own volition, having turned a chapel hour into an unscheduled, through-the-night beginning of the longest running spontaneous revival in Asbury's history.

Before we visited with family in Sarasota and Tampa, we spent three nights at the Avon Park Camp Meeting south of Orlando. On Thursday, February 9, we first learned that something unusual was underway on the campus of our alma mater. Camp President Dr. Tom Hermiz shared from the pulpit that a spontaneous revival had broken out at Asbury University and that we should pray for a mighty work of the Holy Spirit on that campus. From that night until we left Florida for home on February 20, my wife, Darlene, and I were following events in Wilmore as closely as we could through news reports, email, YouTube, and word of mouth. Being a collect-and-preserve-the-sources kind of historian, I scrolled through dozens of accounts on my phone's news apps and emailed many of them to myself for close reading after I returned home.

On Friday afternoon, February 10, Asbury University President Kevin Brown was scheduled to meet in person with Asbury alumni and friends at Avon Park. But an outpouring of God's grace on the Asbury campus intervened. Instead, Dr. Brown shared with us via livestream nonstop singing, students kneeling before a crowded altar in Hughes Auditorium, and the swelling numbers of spiritually hungry pilgrims descending upon Wilmore, having been alerted to Asbury's outpouring by social media.

I confess Darlene and I also hungered to be back in Wilmore. I tried to process how it happened that we were deposited in untimely fashion nine hundred miles from our home, just walking distance from Asbury's campus. It reminded me of my tangential exposure to the Asbury Revival of 1970. I was in my first year of graduate work at the University of Kentucky, seventeen miles from Wilmore. I overheard two anthropology students in UK's King Library talking about some weird religious happening in Wilmore, and they were planning to go check it out. I drove down myself on a Saturday morning and spent hours on a back row in Hughes. There I heard testimony after testimony of lives transformed from students I knew personally who had not been walking with the Lord. I recall in particular the heartfelt, public contrition of one former classmate whom I had known from Trustees Main Dormitory and intramural sports. He was thought to have been burdened by an addiction to pornography, and there he was pledging henceforth a new life in Christ. I was struck by his humility and spiritual transformation. This, I felt confident, was something real.

Returning to 2023 from 1970, even from Florida, Darlene and I were blessed by what we were reading and what we were seeing on YouTube on my tiny phone screen. Upon our return home, we did manage to serve as ushers in Hughes the last three nights of services. Even if only for a few days, I was so thankful I could be a volunteer, one of some fifteen to eighteen hundred over the course of sixteen days. Simultaneously, in my first forty-eight hours back home, I rapidly read through dozens of articles on the revival that I had forwarded to my email account from Florida. I felt doubly blessed—both experiencing the revival's last days firsthand and reading about all sixteen days of this unforgettable spiritual renewal.

Each night when ushering duties were over, I gravitated to my own special niche in Hughes for worship and soul-searching. It was in the back corner near portraits of past Asbury presidents Henry Clay Morrison and Zachary Taylor Johnson. There, God began to work in my own heart as he was working in the hearts of countless others. In particular, for well over a decade I had held a deep well of resentment toward someone at Asbury. I came under conviction to let it go. I wrote this person, who is no longer on campus, asking for forgiveness for my ungodly attitude. This small spiritual victory in my life came to pass through the Holy Spirit's use of a blog post on the revival that included the text of a Fanny Crosby hymn. It broke my hardened heart and led me to repentance:

Pass me not, O gentle Savior,
Hear my humble cry,
While on others Thou art calling,
Do not pass me by.

Savior, Savior,
Hear my humble cry;
While on others Thou art calling,
Do not pass me by.[1]

He did not. On Friday, February 24, 2023, at 8:30 a.m.—weeks later—on YouTube I came across an interview President

Kevin Brown had given on the steps of Hughes Auditorium. He called to mind blind Bartimaeus on the Jericho road. "Have mercy upon me," was the blind man's plea, and the Son of God healed him. Jesus did not pass him by (see Mark 10:46–52).

Even though I was three states away through most of the revival, I had in the back of my mind the thought that I might attempt to write an account of Asbury's spiritual awakening for the benefit of history, but perhaps also for the benefit of those who might read it who are hungering for more of God. Still disappointed over having missed most of the revival in person, of all things a scholarly debate lessened my disappointment. For years a dispute raged in the field of anthropology over the efficacy of studying cultures from inside (emic) versus outside (etic).

Did the perspective of an insider or that of an outsider provide the clearer picture of a people and its culture? Some anthropologists have taken maximalist positions: insiders dismissing the research of outsiders and vice versa. Anthropologist Clifford Geertz has taken a middle tact, arguing that "experience-near" and "experience-distant" observers both provide valuable insights into a people and its culture.[2] For this historian it appeared to be a needless controversy because it seems obvious that the whole truth is best served by firsthand knowledge coupled with insights gleaned from perspectives farther afield. Insider and outsider accounts and sources need not be accorded equal weight, depending upon their reliability, but neither should be ignored.

As regards an understanding of the Asbury Outpouring, the whole truth will best be served by weighing the accounts of insiders (Asburians) and outsiders (visitors to the campus and non-visitors following the outpouring from a distance). Again, not all testimony and not all perspectives are of equal value; all sources have to be judged for their accuracy, asking to what extent they are blessed (or tainted) by their sympathy for (or hostility toward) the Asbury Spiritual Outpouring of 2023.

As for this study's accounting of February 2023, I see myself as mostly an insider, but with some credentials as an outsider as well. On the one hand, I am an insider because I graduated from Asbury College, served on its faculty, and later on its alumni board and board of trustees, in addition to having long-standing family ties to the institution. On the other hand, I have some of the perspective of an outsider. I taught at other institutions nearly twice as long as I taught at Asbury (twenty-three years versus twelve years). Also, as a student of Russian and Ukrainian history, I have studied Eastern Orthodoxy for decades, gaining an appreciation for its strengths and some understanding of its foibles—just as I have long appreciated the strengths and bemoaned the foibles of my own Wesleyan-Holiness tradition.

More specifically, in regard to the Asbury revivals of 1970 and 2023, I see myself as both observer of and imbiber in the blessings of spiritual transformation and renewal. Owing to circumstances of geography, I was nowhere near the center of either the 1970 or 2023 Asbury revivals. At the same time, I believe I have an understanding of Asbury and Wilmore beyond that of a typical outsider. Hopefully, my accounting of the surprise visit of the Holy Spirit to the campuses of Asbury University and Asbury Seminary in February 2023 is better informed because, in varying degrees, I am both an insider and an outsider, one with both "experience-near" and "experience-distant" perspectives, one with hopefully a tolerable degree of both spiritual attachment and historical detachment.

acknowledgments

In researching and writing, we stand on the shoulders of those who have come before us. That is a paraphrase of a sentiment I heard more than once from Dr. Dennis Kinlaw, the president of Asbury College to whom I am indebted on many counts, not least for employment and spiritual counsel.

Immense credit goes to Asbury University President Kevin Brown and Asbury Theological Seminary President Timothy Tennent for their careful and prayerful shepherding of Asbury's spiritual outpouring of 2023, in addition to providing both essential facts and timeless reflections on sixteen unforgettable February days. I am grateful, as well, to Asbury University cabinet members who provided invaluable and voluminous first-hand accounts: Dr. Sarah Baldwin, Glenn Hamilton, Dr. Sherry Powers, Dr. Mark Troyer, and Mark Whitworth.

My interviews with many other Asbury University officials, faculty, and staff helped bring some order to a narrative of an event that in many respects defies human description. Sincere thanks to Brad Atkinson, Jeannie Banter, Greg Haseloff, David Hay, Prof. Heather Hornbeak, Prof. Rob Lim, Equine Center Director and Mayor Harold Rainwater, Prof. David Swartz, and Nathan Vick. Additional informative interviews came from Mark Swayze, David Thomas, the anonymous leader of the

"Consecration Room," and Larry Brown, chair of the university board of trustees.

Blogs proved a valuable source for the book, including three by Asbury Seminary faculty (Craig Keener, Lawson Stone, and Ben Witherington), and Tim Beougher of Southern Baptist Theological Seminary and veteran of the 1995 Wheaton College spontaneous revival. Innumerable conversations added to the narrative, including those with Doug Butler, Jerry Coleman, Jeannette Davis, Keith Madill, Andy Miller, Jonathan Raymond, Steve Seamands (along with other resources), Bud Simon, and Vic Hamilton. In terms of firsthand sources, last but by far not least, are Asbury's Gen Z students, who shared confidentially and candidly such that they should not be thanked by name.

Thanks are in order as well to the fine folk at Seedbed for supporting this project through to print, including J. D. Walt, Andy Miller, Andrew Dragos, Nick Perreault, Maren Kurek, Amanda Varian, Kristin Goble, Tammy Spurlock, and Holly Jones.

Finally, no words in the English language suffice to thank my wife, Darlene Kathryn Montgomery Elliott, for the endless hours she contributed to ushering—and finally kicking—this manuscript out the door.

taken by surprise

introduction

A definitive study of the spiritual awakening that began at Asbury University on February 8, 2023, with a handful of students praying of their own accord following an ordinary chapel service, will come years in the future. Only time will tell how many students—and pilgrims who made the journey to worship at Asbury—came away with lives transformed and repurposed for a lifetime of Christian service. But for the present moment, it is reasonable to conclude that this Asbury revival was real, given how many students and pilgrims went public with their repentance, their resolve to forgive and seek forgiveness, and their reconciliation with God and with those from whom they were estranged. As Asbury University President Kevin Brown has observed, the spiritual awakening that took him by surprise and that for weeks required his every waking hour to affirm and protect, clearly exhibited the fruit of the Spirit: love, joy, peace, patience, kindness, goodness, faithfulness, gentleness, and self-control (Gal. 5:22–23).[1]

The goal of the present study, well short of a comprehensive work, is to record and account for the central features of the spontaneous revival that overtook Asbury University and Asbury Theological Seminary in February 2023 and that had its impact well beyond Wilmore, Kentucky. It is hoped, as well, that *Taken by Surprise* will not only be a preliminary document of record, but that it might serve as an encouragement to readers who seek a closer walk with the Almighty.

Asbury University, like most educational institutions, has lived through its fair share of seasons of administrative, faculty, and student discord. Fortunately and mercifully, these periods of disharmony have often been followed by unexpected visitations of the Holy Spirit, marked by heartfelt repentance, reconciliation, and the institution's reaffirmation of its reason for being: to assist students in their pursuit of academic excellence and spiritual vitality. A constant reminder of the university's rare purpose is the biblical injunction that to this day may be read above the platform in Asbury's Hughes Auditorium: "Holiness unto the Lord."

As examples of the Holy Spirit's restorative powers, take the cases of 1970 and 2023. Prior to the 1970 Asbury Revival, the college was badly fractured, so much so that the preceding four academic years (1965–1969) witnessed a succession of four presidents and an unusually high number of faculty departures— and this in the era of violent protests against the Vietnam War, entrenched white resistance to black civil rights, and a yawning and corrosive Woodstock-versus-Main Street generational divide.[2] Similarly, prior to the campus-wide spiritual renewal of February 2023, Asbury University faced equally divisive challenges, above all COVID-19 and the far-from-optimal educational accommodations the pandemic required. These included the temporary suspension of on-campus classes, followed by the exhausting demands of hybrid classroom/online instruction and the fraught navigation of vaccine and social-distancing protocols. At Asbury, as at other schools across the nation, Gen Zers were at the same time having to cope with heightened levels of anxiety, depression, thoughts of self-harm and suicide, addictions, divisive national politics, culture wars, and gun violence—compounded by too much screen time devoted to smartphones and social media.[3] So the backstories to Asbury's spiritual renewals of 1970 and 2023 set the stage for the fresh wind of God's Spirit that was needed to cleanse and heal broken people and a broken nation.

Robert Kanary, Asbury graduate and author of *Spontaneous Revivals: Asbury College 1905–2006*, was once asked, "'Why Asbury?' I replied, 'Why Abraham, David, or Bethlehem?' In Deuteronomy we read, 'The LORD did not set His love on you nor choose you because you were more in number than any other people, for you were the least of all peoples' (7:7 NKJV)." As Asbury Seminary's Dr. Lawson Stone aptly puts the case: "I just love the way the Spirit washes over this community every generation or so, flushes out a lot of junk, [and] resets the community for fresh obedience."[4]

This language of "*fresh* wind of God's Spirit" and "*fresh* obedience" calls to mind the title of a study that defines revival and awakening as "the restoration of God's people after a period of indifference and decline." It is Keith Hardman's *Seasons of Refreshing: Evangelism and Revivals in America.*[5] Other terms that attempt to capture the experience include *outpouring, awakening, revitalization,* and *renewal.* Still, *refreshing* has its rightful place in the lexicon of the work of the Holy Spirit. Another who employed *refreshing* in his writing was J. Edwin Orr, who spent a lifetime traveling the world documenting the history of revival: "Times of *refreshing* originate in the presence of the Lord. We all desire to see His presence manifested, and we know that God is quite willing to visit us in the power of His own presence."[6] On a trip through Canada in the mid-1930s he composed a hymn, "Cleanse Me," the first verse of which reads:

Lord God, the heavens rend,
Come down and set us free:
A great revival send—
Begin the work in me.[7]

Henry James was a town kid who lived only a stone's throw from the Asbury campus—near where the Miller Communications Building now stands—but would have nothing to do with the college. It was then a surprise to many when he came to saving faith in Asbury's spontaneous revival of 1950, the same one that so empowered Robert Coleman, future professor of evangelism and author of *The Master Plan of Evangelism.* James went on to a faithful life of service in public relations at Asbury College and Asbury Seminary. In *Halls Aflame* he underscored the outward imperative of any true awakening. Speaking of the 1950 outpouring that so radically transformed his own life, he wrote: "Some came to see and experience the *refreshing* of the Lord at Asbury and then went back to their communities to kindle a new flame of revival fire on the altars of their own churches."[8]

Asbury University New Testament Professor Suzanne Nicholson, herself a beneficiary as well as chronicler of Asbury's 2023 outpouring, makes the same point:

> We continue to see famine and poverty, addiction and despair, racism and sexism, abuse and ailments across the world and in our homes. We need this *refreshing* of the Spirit more than ever as a testimony that God has not abandoned this dark world. . . . [But] if we keep this *refreshing* Spirit to ourselves, then we have missed the point.[9]

Thus, a pivotal takeaway looms large: for personal spiritual *refreshing* to be genuine, it must move beyond ourselves to others.

Asbury University was founded by Methodist minister John Wesley Hughes, and Asbury Theological Seminary by Methodist evangelist and publisher Henry Clay Morrison. Nevertheless, neither institution, protective of their Wesleyan-Holiness persuasion, has ever been officially affiliated with the United Methodist Church. The two schools' imperative, "the whole Bible for the whole world," set in stone on the exterior of the university's

Morrison Hall adjacent to Hughes Auditorium, signals a resolve to spread Christian faith both hither and yon. Thus, in keeping with the spirit of Methodism's founder John Wesley and his New World evangelist, Francis Asbury, one mark of authenticity for Asbury's spiritual outpouring of 2023 will be its outward thrust. With the university already responding to more than one hundred requests for student teams to give witness near and far, the campus focus remains in keeping with John Wesley's declaration: "The world is my parish."

one

SPIRITUAL SPONTANEOUS COMBUSTION
February 8

"We closed the chapel at 11:00 this morning, and dozens of students stayed in the room, with a palpable, manifest presence of God. An hour later they are still there." This is how Asbury University Chaplain Greg Haseloff recalls Wednesday, February 8, 2023.[1] That chapel service was one of three held each week at this small Christian liberal arts institution in Wilmore, thirty minutes south of Lexington, Kentucky. President Kevin Brown has described the service that day in Hughes Auditorium as "ordinary" and "unremarkable."[2] That was even the opinion of the morning's speaker, Zach Meerkreebs, Asbury's volunteer assistant soccer coach and Envision Leadership Coordinator for the Christian and Missionary Alliance Church. He had returned home late from a trip the night before and, by his own admission, had had scant time for sermon preparation. After chapel he texted his wife, "I laid a stinker. I'll be home soon."[3] But as the altar filled with students afterward, he realized he would not be home soon.

He had preached on Christlike love, noting the thirty commands to practice it found in just thirteen verses of

Romans 12:9–21. In contrast, he also warned against "radically poor love" that places self above others. He told students, "Some of you guys have experienced that [false] love in the church. Maybe it's not violent, maybe it's not molestation, it's not taken advantage of—but it feels like someone had pulled a fast one on you."[4] The message may not have been remarkable, but it was solidly biblical, certainly heartfelt, and perhaps more convicting than even Pastor Meerkreebs realized, given what shortly followed in its wake. In the final analysis, when he needs to, the God of Scripture can speak to us, no matter the human vessel.

In unforgettable ways, his February 8 chapel message did come to fruition in the coming two weeks of spiritual renewal; it was embedded in soulful singing, in testimonies of deliverance from sin and anxiety, and in earnest teaching and preaching. Central to Asbury's spiritual renewal were themes Pastor Meerkreebs had stressed on February 8: Paul's injunction not to be wise in one's own eyes (radical humility) and the impossibility of fulfilling the thirty love commandments of Romans 12 by one's own efforts. That pivotal morning students were asked how they could "become love." The answer: one has to experience the love of God to become the love of God.[5]

At 10:50 a.m. chapel ended, and most students left for class. But three members of Asbury's largely African American gospel choir lingered to continue singing, along with Asbury staffer Benjamin Black, the group's director and pianist, and several dozen students praying at or near the altar.[6] Gospel choir member Lena Marlowe, a freshman from New Jersey, was on the platform for hours. She recalls, "We just kept singing." It was "very gentle." She was in Hughes that day and night from 10:00 a.m. to 1:00 a.m.; Thursday, noon to 1:00 a.m.; and Friday and Saturday, "all day."[7] Another freshman and fellow member of the gospel choir, Dorcus Lara from Uganda, recalls:

Rev. Zach Meerkreebs preached a sermon about becoming love in action, which I resonated with a lot. When we went up to lead worship again, I just felt God asking me to stay in that moment. I opened up my heart to him and continued to worship sincerely. I remember staying there for an hour after chapel was supposed to end, but then I had to go to my work shift in the IT department.[8]

Asbury senior Charity Johnson, who was also in the gospel choir that morning, noted: "A couple of us were asked to just sing during the altar call, and were singing one of our worship songs. And the worship just never stopped. . . . People just started coming to the altar and just repenting."[9]

When students were dismissed, gospel choir director Benjamin Black and worship leader Georges Dumaine, a Haitian American spouse of a seminary student, gave each other a hug just as student Claire Ferguson slipped in and replaced Benjamin Black at the piano, continuing to accompany gospel choir singers. As University Chapel Coordinator Madeline Black, Benjamin's wife, recalled: "No one was really leading. It was quiet, gentle. I could not leave. I lost track of time."[10]

In the first hour after chapel at the front of Hughes Auditorium, a business major, struggling with both the loss of his parents and a sister in an auto accident the previous year, unburdened himself of sin and made a public confession to those assembled. According to student body president Alison Perfater and Prof. Rob Lim, at that point "the atmosphere changed." Also on February 8, a student made a confession of mean-spiritedness toward many on campus. After also relating memories of abuse in the past, she said, "No one sees me." At that point, a group of her classmates gathered around, embraced her, and prayed with her. Professor Lim remembered: "It was a very powerful moment."[11]

Junior Zeke Atha, among those who had remained, left after an hour to attend his next class on the ground floor of Hughes. Coming out an hour later, he heard singing: "I said, 'Okay, that's weird.' I went back up, and it was surreal. The peace that was in the room was unexplainable." Zeke and several other students then ran from class to class around campus excitedly declaring: "Revival is happening."[12] Others spread the word by texting friends and family.

On a busy day, President Brown had listened to a livestream of chapel from his office, and "the feed just died at 11:00 a.m."[13] Around noon his wife, Maria, texted: "You need to get over here." As he made his way to Hughes he saw a student sprinting toward the building. He later remarked: "That is the image I hope for all students—running to Jesus."[14]

About 11:20 a.m. Zach Meerkreebs forwarded a photo of students still worshipping in Hughes to his longtime mentor, Dr. David Thomas, former senior pastor of Lexington's Centenary United Methodist Church. When around 1:00 p.m. Meerkreebs followed up with a video of students worshipping in Hughes, Dr. Thomas tried to call Zach but could not get through. Sensing something was up, he cancelled his afternoon appointments and drove to Asbury. When Meerkreebs spotted his mentor in Hughes, he immediately went up to him and gave him a hug, shaking all over. The two friends would find themselves devoting many hours over the next sixteen days leading worship from the Hughes platform.[15]

Dr. Sarah Baldwin, vice president of student life, remembers receiving a text at lunch in the cafeteria that Wednesday stating that some students were still praying in Hughes. Students occasionally would linger in prayer after chapel, she knew, but this was different. Soon she found herself engulfed in supporting student-generated worship that seemed to know no end.[16]

One of Asbury Seminary Provost Gregg Okesson's students texted him at 1:00 p.m. that "a revival has broken out in Hughes

Auditorium."[17] About the same time Asbury Seminary President Timothy Tennent was standing in front of a window in his office, directly across Lexington Avenue from the university semicircle and Hughes, when he noticed a student running across the lawn and across the street into the seminary administration building. He excitedly told the president's secretary that chapel never ended that morning.[18]

That same afternoon, across the street at Asbury Seminary, Dr. Jonathan Powers was teaching a course on, of all subjects, worship, when he received a text that something unusual was underway in Hughes Auditorium. He ended up spending hours in Hughes that day and became part of the team that assisted in facilitating worship at the seminary during the revival. That day in class, Dr. Powers had pointed out that knowing about God is different from being with God. A student from his class who also made his way to Hughes that afternoon reminded Dr. Powers that what they were experiencing was just what they had been discussing in class.[19]

In Hughes that afternoon Dr. Jonathan Powers ran into his mother, the university's Provost Sherry Powers. The latter remembered, "When you walked in it was like the presence of the Lord I had never experienced before." She stayed that first night until 8:00 or 8:30 p.m. Those first two days the provost recalled: "A lot of meetings were put on hold," replaced by many meetings shepherding the revival.[20]

That February 8, Dr. Steve Seamands, a retired Asbury Seminary professor, also received a text—this one from his grandson, Andrew, an Asbury junior, telling his grandfather he should come to campus right away. In hindsight, Dr. Seamands, who had been blessed as a senior in the famed Asbury College spontaneous revival of 1970, believes, like Alison Perfater and Rob Lim, that several students opening up and being vulnerable before God and their fellow students was "pivotal."[21]

About 12:20 p.m. Zach Meerkreebs texted Professor Lim that he could not meet him for coffee that afternoon because of ongoing student worship in Hughes. Then students interrupted Lim's 1:00 p.m. class with word of revival. A bit skeptical, he nevertheless dismissed class early, about 1:25, and headed for Hughes. Upon entering he remembered the worship as "gentle, powerful, strong. . . . You could hear students praying and crying." Lim credits the fruit of the outpouring in part to students—and later pilgrims—who were willing to linger for God's leading. In this respect, he and others have even referred to "a theology of lingering."[22]

That afternoon texts kept flying, and students began returning to Hughes in droves. Asbury University New Testament Professor Suzanne Nicholson recalls that first day:

> I wasn't in chapel when the revival started. I had been at the dentist's office with my son. I first heard of this outpouring of the Holy Spirit when a student burst into my introductory New Testament class (located under-neath the auditorium where worship is taking place) at 1:25 that afternoon and declared, "I'm sorry to interrupt, but I don't know if y'all have heard what is happening upstairs—people are *still* worshipping, even though chapel finished three hours ago! The Holy Spirit is moving! Come join us!"[23]

Around 4:30 p.m., with several hundred students now worshipping in Hughes, David Thomas spotted President Brown at the doors leading from the lobby into Hughes proper. Walking up to the president, he said that if there was no dismissal, "I think this could go through the night."[24] At this point Dr. Brown convened an ad hoc meeting of eight administrators and staff downstairs in a ground-floor hallway under the lobby. Present were David Thomas, Sarah Baldwin, Zach Meerkreebs,

Madeline Black, Mark Whitworth, vice president for athletics and communications, Jennifer McChord, vice president for enrollment and marketing, and Jennie Banter, advancement staffer and director of the Christian Life Project. The decision was made to leave Hughes open for worship through the night of February 8–9. Dr. Baldwin proceeded to recruit staff to piece together two-hour shifts through the wee hours, while chapel coordinator Black scrambled to enlist student worship teams to relieve the university gospel choir, which had reassembled the afternoon of February 8 and ended up leading singing for eight to nine hours nonstop.[25]

For this feat of spiritual and physical stamina, Dr. Baldwin sings the praises not only of the singers but of Haitian American Georges Dumaine, an "incredibly gifted worship leader," and gospel choir director Benjamin Black. The spontaneity of student worship that first day impressed Dr. Baldwin, who recalled two students returning to Hughes with a cello and a violin to "praise God with their instruments."[26]

Steve Rehner, Asbury College graduate, former missionary to Colombia, and volunteer student worker, recalls that first day of revival:

> Around 7:00 p.m. I received a text from a student at Asbury who is one of the worship team leaders on campus. She told me that chapel was still going on! I headed over to Hughes Auditorium to see what God was doing, and by then there were hundreds of students in the chapel, and the sense of the Lord's presence was palpable. . . . Very little was being said from the stage, just the worship team leading and those in the auditorium enjoying the warmth, love, and soul rest we felt from the presence of the Lord. Because of this quietness before the Lord, and with the strong sense of the Holy Spirit moving amongst

us, the altar was packed with individuals seeking to confess sin and draw closer to the Lord. I left at 11:00 p.m. that Wednesday night, but there were still hundreds of students worshipping and praising the Lord.[27]

Dr. Nicholson vividly remembers her own personal soul-searching those first hours of worship on February 8:

> I confess that I struggled that first day because I had been carrying some personal burdens . . . and I was afraid that once God started working on my heart I would be undone, a weeping puddle on the floor of Hughes Auditorium. So that first day I went upstairs for just a few minutes to see what God was doing. It certainly appeared that God was moving. The praise was genuine, the prayers unforced. . . . When I went home that evening, I continued to feel a remarkable spirit of joy and peace. It was so refreshing! As the revival has continued, I often wake up in the middle of the night with the music and lyrics of praise flowing through my head—not my normal experience.[28]

The heart of what transpired at Asbury February 8–23 was worship. Many present those days recall an extraordinary sense of being in communion with God, often immediately upon entering Hughes Auditorium or one of the overflow venues. Evangelist Jerry Coleman of the Wilmore-based Francis Asbury Society served as an altar counselor every day for two weeks. He shared that many worshippers told him upon entering Hughes or Estes Chapel or McKenna Chapel, "They immediately sense[d] God's deep Spirit of peace and unity."[29] Eric Allen, Kentucky Baptist Convention missions team leader, was in Hughes with his wife, Sherry, Saturday night, February 11: "We had only been there a few minutes singing music when we were both moved emotionally and in tears because the presence of God was so real in that place."[30] Bill Elliff, founding pastor of The Summit Church in North Little Rock, Arkansas, has written extensively on revival. In Hughes on February 10, he noted: "Within the first hour, I had moved from a spectator to a humble participant. . . . You don't want to leave."[31]

Professor Tim Beougher of Louisville's Southern Seminary and pastor of West Broadway Baptist Church has also written a great deal on revival, including *Accounts of a Campus Revival: Wheaton College 1995*. In Hughes on February 13, he said: "I experienced that same overwhelming sense of God's presence each day/night during the 1995 Wheaton Revival."[32] Asbury Seminary Provost Gregg Okesson, also working at Wheaton in 1995, drew parallels between the two outpourings including an "insatiable hunger for Christ" and "acute spiritual sensitivity."[33] Asbury Seminary Professor Tom McCall recalled the same: "Anyone who has spent time in Hughes Auditorium over the past few days can testify that this promised Comforter is present and powerful. I cannot analyze—or even adequately describe—all that is happening, but there is no doubt in my mind that God is present and active."[34]

Katie Reynolds, who is a volunteer youth worker at Lexington's Pax Christi Catholic Church, made the fifteen-mile trek to Wilmore three times with her four children, ages six to eighteen. She noted on February 10: "I took our kids after a basketball game on Friday night at 9:00 p.m. . . . Every seat [in Hughes] was full, and it was standing room only. You could feel the Holy Spirit in the building." Her thirteen-year-old son, Dylan, said, "It was really powerful and so cool to see everyone praising [God]." His six-year-old sister, Lucy, said the singing made her feel as if "Jesus was right next to me."[35]

The next day, February 11, Larry Brown, chair of the university board of trustees, was on the last row of the balcony looking down across the expanse of worshippers and the crowded altar.

He shared that he had never seen so many people at once so dearly intent on a time with God. That was his "best moment," just watching what the Lord was doing.[36] After "a season at Hughes Auditorium," Asbury Seminary Old Testament Professor Lawson Stone likened the sensation to the relief after a long hike of finding "a lovely, cool stream" where he "just peeled off my shoes and socks and let my hot, sore feet soak in the water."[37] A week into the nonstop worship, Asbury Seminary President Timothy Tennent shared:

> There comes a point when the people of God become tired of casual prayers and move to that point of desperation which opens us up in fresh ways to God's surprising work. That is what I have experienced most over the past week in my own life. . . . I have been in Hughes Auditorium or Estes, or both, every day and night, and it is like stepping into a flowing spiritual river. You sense the presence and power of God working in people's lives. Since last Wednesday when the outpouring began, I have reflected many times on Jesus' statement about the Spirit when he said, "The wind blows wherever it wants. Just as you can hear the wind but can't tell where it comes from or where it is going, so you can't explain how people are born of the Spirit" [John 3:8 NLT].[38]

two

THE BACKSTORY
2023 in Context

Past Asbury Revivals

Occasions of spontaneous, student-generated, through-the-night worship and spiritual renewal are nothing new to Asbury. Its students have been witnesses to memorable visitations of the Holy Spirit in their midst, lasting extended hours or days, in 1905, 1908, 1921, 1950, 1958, 1970, 1992, 2006, and now 2023.[1] Before 2023 arguably the most notable Asbury revivals were 1905, out of which came E. Stanley Jones, missionary statesman, evangelist, and writer of devotional classics—perhaps Asbury's most acclaimed graduate;[2] 1950, which deeply impacted Robert E. Coleman, future seminary professor and author of *The Master Plan of Evangelism* (with sales approaching four million copies and translations into one hundred languages);[3] 1958, which included the participation of student leader Paul Rader, later general of the Salvation Army and president of Asbury College;[4] and 1970, which changed the life trajectory of countless students who dedicated their lives to Christian service.[5] Paul Prather, religion writer for the *Lexington Herald-Leader*, seems to have it right: "Revivalism is baked into Asbury's DNA."[6]

Firsthand accounts of the 1970 Asbury Revival, which ran for 185 hours,[7] are best captured in Robert Coleman's anthology, *One Divine Moment*. Asbury Seminary Old Testament Professor Lawson Stone recalls: "Reading this book sealed my decision to come to Asbury, and I ended up marrying the daughter of the author!"[8] Speaking of the 1970 Revival, Asbury College President Dennis Kinlaw told his board: "This act of God" was "undeserved but deeply desired . . . a gift for which one can only bow in humble, grateful praise."[9] Asbury University is noted for its Wesleyan persuasion, its reverence for its namesake Methodist horseback-riding bishop Francis Asbury, and in the words of *Christianity Today*'s Daniel Silliman, its "tradition of revivals and a theology that teaches people to wait and watch for a divine wind to blow."[10]

Previous American and Global Spiritual Awakenings

Still, students of church history and the Bible will know that neither Asbury nor the wider Wesleyan movement have any corner on startling periods of spiritual renewal that have been deep and wide. In the American religious experience one can point to the First Great Awakening (1730–1770); the Second Great Awakening (1795–1835), including the oft-noted Cane Ridge Revival of 1801 (like Asbury, in Central Kentucky); the Azusa Street Revival of 1906 that launched the Pentecostal movement; and the Jesus Revolution of the 1970s, with a feature film of the same name released in the same month as the Asbury 2023 Outpouring.[11]

Farther afield, author J. Edwin Orr spent a lifetime documenting global spiritual renewals similar to Asbury's experience, including the Children's Revival in Silesia (1707–1708), the Welsh Revival (1904), the Shantung Revival (1927–1937), the Hebrides Revival (1949–1953), and the West Timor Revival (1965), to name just a few.[12] And as for denominational persuasion, the winds of the Spirit have been no respecter of particular theological persuasions, instead at different times blessing Anabaptists, Puritans, Pietists, Presbyterians, Methodists, Baptists, and Pentecostals.[13]

Reaching still further back, being filled with the Holy Spirit is hardly an obscure occurrence in Christian Scripture. Accounts of this spiritual blessing are recorded at least nineteen times (twice in Exodus, once in Deuteronomy, once in Micah, four times in Luke, ten times in Acts, and once in Ephesians).[14] Yet some observers of the Asbury Revival of 2023, perhaps unaware of spiritual awakenings as commonplace in church history, appear either bewildered by or hostile to what they learn of it.[15] What some cannot fathom is why Gen Z youth, easily the most irreligious US demographic cohort,[16] would be susceptible to a spiritual awakening such as occurred at Asbury in February 2023 and on other campuses and churches in its wake. Part of the explanation may be found in the weight of anxiety today's teens and early twenties carry with them in their backpacks.

On the Eve: An Anxious Age

Christian counselors may point us in the right direction, seeing revival as a response to unsettled times. On Martin Luther King Jr. Day, January 16, 2023, I met Daniel Lee at an interracial breakfast in Nicholasville, Kentucky, seven miles from Wilmore and Asbury. He is the founder and director of two counseling services based in Lexington and Louisville and pastor of the African American Marble Creek Baptist Church. At 6'7" and around three hundred pounds, this former University of Kentucky lineman makes a commanding impression. During that meal I asked Pastor Lee what had changed the most over the decades he had been engaged in counseling. Without hesitation, he answered it was his clients' heightened level of anxiety. Just days later I shared this observation with Asbury University Chaplain Greg Haseloff, who immediately concurred. Many youth today, including youth at Christian colleges and universities, are having to deal with some combination of addictions, family turmoil, not measuring up to the perfect bodies and affluence of advertisements, loneliness, feelings of worthlessness and depression, suicidal thoughts, a decline in civil discourse (especially in politics), and too much time devoted to social media and its increasingly confrontational and vicious repartee.[17]

In 2020, psychologist Jean M. Twenge of San Diego State University reported that large national studies over the previous decade that focused on American youth had documented decreased levels of happiness and life satisfaction and increased loneliness, anxiety, depression, hospital admissions for self-harm behaviors, and suicide. The same decade also saw an increase in adolescent smartphone ownership and social media activity, from more than 50 percent in 2021 to 80–81 percent by 2023. Studies indicate that adolescents' increasing use of smartphones and time spent on social media interfere with sleep and in-person social interaction and facilitate cyberbullying and greater access to self-harm information. Youth wrapped up in their phones and favored social media platforms often enter nearly secretive echo chambers of predation which encourage harmful practices and ideas. Dr. Twenge's conclusion is that the US is "in the midst of a mental health crisis among adolescents . . . particularly among girls and young women." A growing consensus among health-care specialists is that this "decline in mental health may be linked . . . to the increasing popularity of smartphones and social media."[18]

Summarizing the rise in adolescent angst, *New York Times* writer Ruth Graham notes Gen Zers have "been battered by everything from political polarization to COVID-19 shutdowns to a near epidemic of depression."[19] All of these destructive trends have been compounded by pandemic-enforced online learning and isolation. COVID-related stressors have been hard enough for adults, but for preteens, teens, and college-age youth, they have been especially debilitating. For Professor David Swartz, the first few days of Asbury's spiritual awakening "felt like a long exhale taken by anxious students reeling from the pressures of COVID-19 and social media—and then an infilling of a holy calm."[20]

Lexington Herald-Leader columnist Paul Prather notes that some want to see revivals as "reactions to major social upheavals . . . when we're rattled. . . . Others see them as merciful visitations from God, who cares about people and occasionally shows up in especially dramatic ways to let us know it." He adds, in fact, both can be true.[21] Mike Allen, an Asbury Seminary graduate and director of family life and evangelization for the Catholic Diocese of Lexington, spent time at the Asbury Revival on February 14. He observed: "People are hungry and longing for intimacy, community. Young people (in particular) have been through a really difficult time due to the pandemic, and it will be a while before we fully unpack that experience."[22]

According to Asbury junior Dakota Poole, "We're learning how to love across greater boundaries and rifts. We're learning about the effort Love takes. If God is Love, and He crosses boundaries, we're called to do the same." Alexandra Presta, editor of the *Collegian* campus newspaper, recalls:

> I remember Asbury during 2020. Not only did the coronavirus keep us physically apart, but there were a lot of cliques based on majors, athletics, political preferences, and more. The enemy thrived on this division. Our loving God fought against it; He is a God of unity. Why else would His Spirit fall on a bunch of students on a random Wednesday morning?[23]

Asbury University Director of Communications Abby Laub thought she would never see a spiritual outpouring like the one

Asbury experienced in 1970. "But here it is. And it just gives me so much hope that this next generation, this Gen Z generation, does not have to be defined by anxiety, but they can be defined by hope."[24] From the platform in Hughes, Vice President Sarah Baldwin recalled: "Many testimonies from college students about release from anxiety, depression, suicidal ideation. Come Lord Jesus! This generation needs this."[25]

On the Eve: Prayers for Renewal

In February 2023 the spiritual renewal at Asbury University and across the street at Asbury Theological Seminary was by all accounts spontaneous and unplanned. At the same time, the anxieties and malaise of unsettled, divisive times were a harbinger helping explain students suddenly crying out to God for help and mercy. Another prerequisite to February 8, 2023, were the prayers for spiritual renewal that had been lifted up for years. Just as prior to the 1958 and 1970 Asbury revivals, there were students who had committed to a regimen of spiritual disciplines called "The Great Experiment," which included daily prayers for a new work of God's grace on campus.[26]

Less programmatic but as heartfelt were the prayers for a spiritual outpouring offered up by Mary Hosteller, a freshman intercultural studies major from Pennsylvania. She and a classmate met in Hughes for an hour of prayer before classes Monday through Wednesday, February 6–8.[27] In the same vein, Asbury Seminary Professor Tom McCall relates: "Several current students and recent alumni tell me that for several years they have been praying together for a move of God, and they are thrilled beyond words to see what is happening."[28] Others praying for a fresh outpouring of the Holy Spirit included Asbury Seminary Professor Steve Seamands (every Friday in Estes Chapel at

2:00 p.m. for five years in a small group) and Seedbed ministry's J. D. Walt and David Thomas (for seven years).[29]

Professor Craig Keener, a widely respected biblical scholar on the Asbury Seminary faculty, also had seminarians share with him their anticipation and prayers for spiritual renewal, and he heard the same from Zach Meerkreebs who spoke in the February 8 chapel. Keener relates: "I meant to be supportive of these expectations. But as years passed, I wondered if an outpouring of the Spirit would happen on any significant scale while I was still here. . . . I was hoping it would happen before I retired."[30] So, in sum, the hour that the mercies of the Holy Spirit might once again be poured out upon the likes of Asbury was unknown, but many in the Asbury community and among its graduates were praying in anticipation to that end.

three

THE HEART OF WORSHIP
Unpolished and Quiet—as Compliments

Music

The Asbury Outpouring of February 2023 had all the traditional hallmarks of a genuine spiritual revival: prayers (before and during), preaching, teaching, repentance, confession, reconciliation; for some, a witness to new life in Christ; and, for others, a deeper walk in faith through the ministry of the Holy Spirit. But for this writer it was the music in Hughes Auditorium that was the Holy Spirit's catalyst into my heart. Like others recalling first entering the auditorium that month, the voices of fifteen hundred souls lifting praise to God struck a deep spiritual chord. During summer Asbury reunions, I have especially looked forward to Friday night hymn sings in Hughes Auditorium. Similarly, the most memorable aspect of the music of the February 2023 outpouring was vocal. With no organ, and with piano and guitar decidedly subdued in the background, it was simple choruses sung by fifteen hundred earnest, hungry worshippers that God used to speak to my soul in a way I will never forget.

So it was music, mostly praise choruses and occasional hymns, that set the tone for worship, February 8–23. Baptist seminary Professor Laura Levens noted:

Singing and prayer were the central practices, and the songs pleaded for stripping away all other matters except pursuit of experience with God. People speak of the Asbury Revival as spontaneous and ecumenical, and it is so because people attending abide the various ways the people next to them are pursuing God in prayer and song.[1]

Deeply moved, Asbury University New Testament Professor Suzanne Nicholson wrote:

The worship in Hughes has been joyful and unforced. . . . The musicians—many of whom are my students—seamlessly replace one another on stage to give each other rest breaks. It's like passing the baton in a relay race. I am so proud of them! There is no need for a single leader and no competition to be on stage.[2]

"This encounter with God," sophomore Dorcus Lara shared, "reminded me of Uganda . . . There is not usually a PowerPoint up telling you what songs to sing or a strict time constraint. It's just you and the worship leader being filled with the power of God."[3]

Asbury administrators worked hard to facilitate worship that remained as much as possible as it had begun after chapel February 8. Voices sang praise to the Lord, with instrumentalists keen not to draw attention to themselves: a single cajon instead of a drum set, piano but no organ, one or two acoustic guitars at most—all at a low decibel compared to typical contemporary worship and Christian concerts.[4] This writer's observation is that you could *hear* the singing, and it was both melodious and spiritually moving. Others, as well, upon first entering Hughes Auditorium, were struck by the swell of voices not overpowered by instruments.

Chaplain Greg Haseloff shared that the worship teams were often "unflashy and unpolished," but it was not meant as a criticism because performance was not the goal; the goal was worship, pure and simple. The chaplain saw it as part of an arc in worship music over decades in which many churches are moving away from spectacle, "coming back to the heart of worship."[5]

J. D. Walt is leader of Tennessee-based, Asbury Seminary–affiliated Seedbed, whose mission is "to gather, connect, and resource the people of God to sow for a Great Awakening." Present in Hughes Auditorium during the outpouring, he recalled: "In one of the late-night sessions one of the students began to lead the house in singing the simple chorus, 'Sanctuary.' We will sing it together again today: 'Lord, prepare me to be a sanctuary, pure and holy, tried and true. With thanksgiving, I'll be a living sanctuary for you.'"[6]

Prior to February 2023, this writer favored traditional hymns in worship, jokingly making light of "7/11" choruses, seven words repeated eleven times. But in Hughes, as noted, the calm, reverential student preferment for simple words of adoration of the Lord melted my soul. A few words or many words—it did not matter to me. Dr. Steve Seamands commented on the worshipful atmosphere students on the platform engendered through their singing, even with the most spartan of lyrics, such as the prayerful intoning of "Agnus Dei" for an hour.[7] Daniel Silliman, reporting for *Christianity Today*, wrote that as one midnight of worship approached,

> A young woman in an oversized gray sweatshirt that read "Zionsville" raised one hand to heaven and led the students in singing Chris Tomlin's "How Great Is Our God." "The Godhead three in one," she sang. "Father, Spirit, Son. . . . How great is our God? Sing with me." More than 1,000 students did, raising their hands and lifting their voices. The surge of their worship filled the chapel to the rafters, overwhelming the thin audio of the

livestream. "How Great Is Our God," they sang. "All will see how great, how great is our God."[8]

Gen Z to the Fore

From the outset President Kevin Brown sought to privilege students in making decisions regarding the revival. They, after all, first demonstrated the work of the Holy Spirit in launching days of repentance, getting right with God, and getting right with each other. Once over the initial surprise of a spontaneous spiritual awakening, President Brown and his leadership team purposed to support Asbury's students in their central role in leading worship. Revival participant Nick Hall of Minneapolis-based Pulse ministry gave pride of place to Asbury students: Gen Z youth were "the ones that started it, they're the ones that sustained it, and they're the ones that have been on the platform the whole time."[9]

Asbury Seminary biblical studies scholar Craig Keener was quick to let Paul Prather of the *Lexington Herald-Leader* know that he was not a leader, but rather one who supported the outpouring in prayer and worship: "It started with the students. I think they're the most important component."[10] Asbury administrators and faculty readily affirmed students who led in initiating revival. As altar counselor Steve Rehner put it: "The goal has been for no administrators or leaders to take limelight, only for Jesus to be glorified."[11] Many observers were struck by what they perceived as "radical humility." One African American mother and minister who traveled with her family from Columbus, Ohio, remarked, "There were no celebrity praise leaders. There were no famous names giving addresses. There was nothing for people to go there [for] . . . other than the presence of God and what they felt God was doing in this place."[12]

Southern Baptist Seminary Professor Tim Beougher appreciated that "the worship leaders did what worship leaders should do—they were not performers, but led us to the throne of grace in worship."[13] "I know none of their names," commented Professor Laura Levens, "because they weren't introduced. Hence Asbury's claim it is a revival without a name." In the same vein, Seedbed's J. D. Walt shared: "Nobody has a clue who anybody is [up front]. This is not a platform moment."[14] Pastor Bill Elliff came to the same conclusion: "Worship is being led by various student teams. Some more proficient than others, but all are humble. We do not know their names. There are no fog machines nor lights—just piano and guitar by unnamed students worshipping God."[15] J. D. Walt again: "There is not a shred of production in any of it." Worship and worship leaders are "impressively unimpressive."[16] Ditto for volunteer worship team facilitator Mark Swayze from Houston: "So who are these college worship leaders at the Asbury Outpouring? Who sits on the 'Worship Steward' team? You will never know. They are a nameless and faceless generation. They are rebelling against the celebrity culture infiltrating the church."[17] How ironic it was for members of this generation, so bedeviled and perhaps fatigued by the "influencer" culture of social media, to reject it as they led worship in Asbury's spiritual awakening.

As Lexington Catholic youth worker Katie Reynolds put it, worship leaders were "seeking zero attention."[18] Thomas Lyons of Northern Seminary observed firsthand: "The stage is largely empty, with worship teams off to the side. The altar railing is full without hyped-up altar calls, and people come to kneel at it as the Holy Spirit prompts them."[19] Some well-known Christian personalities did come without fanfare and sat on the hard wooden seats of Hughes Auditorium like everyone else. Seminary Provost Gregg Okesson was aware that the university turned down a number of marquee Christian musicians who volunteered to perform at no charge. But performance was not what Asbury's Gen Z youth were seeking. Celebrities who came unbidden anyway "were kindly told they could come to the altar and receive prayer. Many did precisely that."[20] Daniel Silliman of *Christianity Today* reported some notables "went quietly, just to pray and participate without trying to take the stage. Kari Jobe, the contemporary Christian music singer who won a Dove Award for 'The Blessing' in 2021, went to Asbury and went down to the altar. Several students prayed for her, according to Asbury staff, without appearing to know who she was. A leader of the Vineyard Church came and went without announcing anything on social media."[21]

This writer was told of other prominent Christian artists, bishops, and denominational executives who were never introduced and who simply worshipped with everyone else. These "Christian celebrities," as Dr. Sarah Baldwin put it, came "unannounced and without introduction or without crowd awareness." She continued:

> Somewhere early in this . . . without talking to each other about it at first—we just stopped introducing ourselves at the mic . . . (with the exception of the actual 10:00–11:00 chapel hours, M/W/F). Nameless. It just seemed unimportant to even say our names. When we coordinate so very carefully introductions all throughout the year at AU, now it has just been about Jesus.[22]

One prominent East Coast pastor, previously scheduled to speak in the university chapel, was introduced—albeit sparingly—by first name only.[23]

Daniel Silliman observed that when Asbury faculty and staff and a few others did deliver messages, they often "didn't stop to say their own names or job titles, instead reminding worshippers, 'There are no celebrities here, no superstars, except Jesus.'"[24] Northern Seminary Professor Thomas Lyons recalled:

I watched world-class biblical scholars usher people to open seats and the university's president introduce himself by saying, "Hi, my name is Kevin. I work here at Asbury." And although scholars and presidents are serving the community, the core of this movement, both its leadership and target audience, is the Gen Z students who have been present since the beginning.[25]

Simple and Quiet

New Testament Professor Nicholson related that "Stereotypes of big personalities and manufactured power" did not fit the picture of worship in Hughes Auditorium: "As I sat and listened to the worship, I wept as God lifted my burdens, and I rejoiced at the sweet, gentle Spirit of the Lord. This was not what I had expected when I heard students running down the hallway the day before proclaiming, 'There's a revival going on upstairs!'"

According to Pastor Bill Elliff:

If you have the privilege of visiting Asbury during these days, you will be shocked by how quiet it often is. Hours of simple worship, interspersed by silence. There are great moments of joyful singing, testimony, preaching, joy. But there are hours through the night and early mornings of waiting on God. The room has been soaked in humble prayers for days. . . . The Bible calls this "awe." It is always present when God comes. "The Lord is in His holy temple. Let all the earth keep silent" (Hab. 2:20).[26]

NBC News quoted another outside observer to the effect, "This is as un-sensationalized as it could be." According to the NBC reporters on hand, "The setup is simple. No projector screens or high-tech integrations, just wooden sanctuary chairs filled with people, and an open altar call with an invitation to prayer that [as of February 15] still hasn't ended."[27] According to Adam Russell, director of Vineyard Worship (USA), "It's not even low production—it's no production," and he meant it as a compliment.[28]

Here is the reflection of Baptist Seminary Professor Laura Levens, who drove down to Asbury from Lexington:

> I visited the revival at Asbury University on Tuesday, February 14. I arrived mid-morning, and when I entered Hughes Chapel, the entire crowd was bathed in soft, golden light. Two-story, buttery yellow stained glass windows cast everything and everyone with a serene glow like an eternal sunset. . . . Everything on stage was an intentionally low-fi production during my two-and-a-half hour stay. Three people were on stage singing and playing music. They gently rocked and sang softly as they played guitar and piano. A large drum kit and the stately organ pipes went unused.[29]

Northern Seminary's Thomas Lyons, who lives in Lexington, was profoundly moved by his time in Hughes Auditorium:

> Despite the claims that what is happening at Asbury is simply "heightened emotional connection," my direct observations suggest it is nothing of the sort. The environment I have observed is positively muted compared to many charismatic contexts I've worshipped in. The general response has been a hushed, deep reverence for the tangible presence of God that is being experienced in that place. I have heard others who have experienced it the past couple days describe it as a "deep peace" and the "quiet, heavy presence of God."[30]

Asbury altar counselor Steve Rehner also recalled the Holy Spirit's quiet work:

It has been said that "the wild thing about what is happening at Asbury is that it is not wild at all!" I like that a great deal. Because it has simply been the quiet moving of the Holy Spirit, moving as His children, and seekers, sit and bask in His presence. While we are quiet before Him, He has been able to move people to go deeper.[31]

University faculty member Christel Broady, who teaches English as a second language (ESL), told a reporter what was happening in worship was "anything but sensationalistic—quite the opposite . . . To see all these young people in reverent worship, quiet and . . . giving God the glory, made me so happy, as a Catholic, as a mother, as a teacher."[32]

Calm and Serene

Leaders of both Asbury institutions have characterized the climate of spiritual renewal in their midst as calm and serene. According to Asbury University President Kevin Brown, "Since the first day, there have been countless expressions and demonstrations of radical humility, compassion, confession, consecration, and surrender unto the Lord." He liked how one person put it: sometimes in Hughes one seemed to be part of "a Holy Hush."[33] Similarly, Asbury Theological Seminary President Timothy Tennent noted that what was:

> regularly observed by those who have been a regular part of these services is the solemnity and peace in the various places where this movement has spread around town. Sometimes we envision "revivals" as times when people hear fiery sermons and there are big outbursts of emotion. This move of God is marked more by quiet weeping than emotive shouting.[34]

One of Dr. Tennent's faculty members, theology professor Tom McCall, with a son and daughter enrolled at Asbury University, shared with *Christianity Today*:

> As an analytic theologian, I am weary of hype and very wary of manipulation. I come from a background (in a particularly revivalist segment of the Methodist-holiness tradition) where I've seen efforts to manufacture "revivals" and "movements of the Spirit" that were sometimes not only hollow but also harmful. I do not want anything to do with that.
>
> And truth be told, this is nothing like that. There is no pressure or hype. There is no manipulation. There is no high-pitched emotional fervor.
>
> To the contrary, it has so far been mostly calm and serene. The mix of hope and joy and peace is indescribably strong and indeed almost palpable—a vivid and incredibly powerful sense of *shalom*. The ministry of the Holy Spirit is undeniably powerful but also so gentle. . . .
>
> What we are experiencing now—this inexpressibly deep sense of peace, wholeness, holiness, belonging, and love—is only the smallest of windows into the life for which we are made.[35]

Sarah Marshall, a former Asbury University student from West Virginia, returned to campus within days of hearing of through-the-night worship on campus:

> This was an invitation to experience Him and I accepted. I felt a relaxation and calmness like I have never experienced before. A stillness went throughout the chapel, and I couldn't help but be fully present and attuned to God's presence. There is holy ground alive at Asbury and God's spirit is there!! I have no words to describe the worship. Indescribable worship. He was there.[36]

A returning Asbury Seminary grad was struck by what seemed like a lack of human agency: "I was impressed with how intentional everyone seemed to be to not demand any particular feeling or response to what was taking place. Gentleness, submission, and meekness permeated the attitude of the space and those who had leadership roles throughout our time there."[37]

Time Stood Still

The Wilmore United Methodist Church has had close ties with the Asbury institutions throughout its existence. Prominent in the sanctuary, completed in 1964, is a stained glass window of Christ and these three words: "Come, Tarry, Go." That middle injunction—tarry—was a much-remarked-upon feature of the Asbury Revival 2023. Worship speaker David Thomas recalled: "We embraced lingering . . . cracking the code of Gen Z . . . no pressure, no marketing, willingness to be interrupted, clearing calendars."[38] Keith Madill, an Asbury College graduate and retired school administrator, was a volunteer on campus during the extended worship services. His son Isaac told his father that, while sitting in Hughes Auditorium, time seemed to fly by. Hours seemed like minutes.[39] In the same vein, Thomas Lyons reported:

> People are moved by the tangible presence of God to linger in that place for hours (and even days) on end. . . . In our hurry-filled, over-scheduled Western American culture whose obsession with productivity, achievement, and consumerism has saturated every corner of life, life has simply ground to a halt in this little corner of Kentucky so that people can prioritize spending time soaking in the manifest presence of God.[40]

Asbury Seminary Professor Tom McCall told *Christianity Today*:

Many people say that in the chapel they hardly even realize how much time has elapsed. It is almost as though time and eternity blur together as heaven and earth meet. Anyone who has witnessed it can agree that something unusual and unscripted is happening. . . .

The holy love of the triune God is apparent, and there is an inexpressible sweetness and innate attractiveness to it. It is immediately obvious why no one wants to leave and why those who must leave want to come back as soon as they can.[41]

Mixing firsthand observation with preaching mode, Arkansas Pastor Bill Elliff contends:

One of the reasons we see little of God is that we do not give Him time. Asbury has been fueled by students who are willing to give God hours, even through the night. There is much in Scripture about waiting on God that we don't understand because we think everything depends on our fast-paced human work. . . . The revival here [at Asbury] is not hurried or rushed. There are long periods of stillness and waiting. If you want to rush in, get a big dose of God and rush out, don't come. God works on His timetable. We give God little time and almost no silence. What is happening here is occurring because thirsty people are waiting before God.

For Elliff what is needed is to "tarry before God (not social media)."[42]

Asbury Seminary New Testament Professor Ben Witherington well captured the calm, serene aura and the life-changing work of the Spirit:

What exactly is happening inside Hughes? Singing, testimony, and other sorts of speaking and Scripture reading, and what can best be characterized as a sweet, gentle spirit of love, repentance, forgiveness, peace, and a clear sense of the presence of the Lord. . . . I doubt those participating will ever be the same after this, and certainly they will never forget this unplanned, spontaneous visit of the Spirit.[43]

four

TRANSFORMED IN WORSHIP
Dying to Self

Repentance and Forgiveness

Jerry Coleman, who served at the altar in Hughes Auditorium for many days on end, reported "People accepting Jesus for the first time, others surrendering their wills and inviting the Holy Spirit to fill them," with others "experiencing deep, deep peace with God."[1] Dr. David Thomas, serving on the platform and at the altar throughout the outpouring, was particularly moved by the work of Christ in the life of a Hindu penitent from India. She came to the altar without preaching or a specific call to repentance, and with tears flowing down her face, she told Dr. Thomas, "I have met Him." "Are there things in your life for which you need to repent?" he asked. "I want to repent of everything," she replied.[2]

Freshman Dorcus Lara had just as profound an experience through the February weeks of spiritual renewal:

> The Holy Spirit has brought healing in my heart from past trauma where I put up a wall and didn't want to address. But throughout the prayers, God has helped me open those wounds. Throughout the time of revival, multiple people have approached me to pray over me, and

they would remind me that I am worthy and loved by God. Those words seem simple, and you think that every Christian would know that, but sometimes because of the hurt you experience and sins you've committed you forget that you are still loved by God.[3]

Southern Seminary Professor Tim Beougher, author of a study of the 1995 Wheaton College revival, asks and answers the question:

How do we know if what we think might be a revival is a genuine work of God? One unmistakable sign will be repentance. J. Edwin Orr, the great historian of revival, once remarked that we really don't understand what we are praying for when we pray for revival—we think we are praying for ecstasy, and yes, joy is a by-product of revival. But true revival doesn't begin in ecstasy, it begins with agony. It doesn't begin with laughter but with tears. The Bible teaching [in Hughes Auditorium] this afternoon and several of the testimonies focused on repentance— not just feeling sorry for our sin but with the Lord's help seeking to remove it as far as we can from our lives.[4]

Asbury Collegian editor Alexandra Presta reported that at the very beginning of the revival:

During a call of confession, at least a hundred people fell to their knees and bowed at the altar. Hands rested on shoulders, linking individual people together to represent the Body of Christ truly. Cries of addiction, pride, fear, anger, and bitterness sounded, each followed by a life-changing proclamation: "Christ forgives you."[5]

Asbury ESL Professor Christel Broady recalled that "the sight of students 'suddenly kneeling together . . . arm in arm'" brought her to tears.[6] On February 7 in a classroom on the ground floor of Hughes Auditorium the subject was Acts 3 in Professor Nicholson's Growth of the New Testament Church class, in particular, Peter's speech after he had performed a healing near the Jerusalem Temple: "Repent therefore, and turn to God so that your sins may be wiped out, so that times of refreshing may come from the presence of the Lord" (Acts 3:19–20a NRSV). Nicholson recalled: "Our class had discussed the beauty of the description, 'times of refreshing,' only to experience that refreshing the very next day!"[7]

Ruth Graham, onsite at Asbury writing for the *New York Times*, reported that accounts of healing were "overwhelmingly about mental health, trauma, and disillusionment."[8] Father Norman Fischer is an African American priest at Lexington's St. Peter Claver Church and chaplain at Lexington Catholic High School. He made his way to Asbury following his Sunday mass, February 12, and spotted some of his current and former LCHS students in Hughes. He related that he rather quickly "got into praise mode." What was happening at Asbury he considered "definitely of God, definitely of the Holy Spirit." Father Fischer ended up hearing confessions and offering "healing prayers for some attendees—including one young man struggling with addiction."[9]

To the same point, Asbury Seminary President Tennent noted that in an overflow chapel on the seminary campus "the vast majority of testimonies were of addictions that were broken." University Chaplain Greg Haseloff remembered that it was a student repenting at the altar after chapel on February 8 that had set the revival in motion. And that, he remarked, "is not, unfortunately, a common practice in our churches these days."[10]

Without question an essential corollary to repentance is forgiveness. Asbury College graduate and retired United Methodist pastor Robert Kanary is the author of the most comprehensive anthology on Asbury revivals to date. As he puts it, "Invariably there is a sense of God's incredible and tangible presence. Among other features, hallmarks are intense hunger for God, people getting right with God, getting right with each other, forgiving and forgetting past offenses."[11] Asbury Seminary New Testament scholar Ben Witherington, reflecting on the Asbury Outpouring, makes clear that:

> Revivals . . . involve serious repentance of sin . . . And repentance leads to the pronouncement of forgiveness, and rightly so. Christ has already paid for those sins, past, present, and future, but, to appropriate the benefits of that atonement, one needs to repent. And there are also opportunities not merely to receive forgiveness from God, but to offer it to others who may have hurt or sinned against you. Read Matthew 18. Christ says we must forgive *ad infinitum*—he even says 77 times or 7 times 70 depending on how one reads the Greek. And interestingly this number only shows up one other time in Scripture—Lamech in Genesis says he will take revenge that many times. So Christ has come to stop revenge-taking, stop the violence, stop the hatred, and remind people in the prayer he gave his disciples "forgive us our trespasses as we forgive those who trespass against us."[12]

Repentance, confession, and forgiveness may or may not be accompanied by bells and whistles, fireworks, and signs and wonders. In February 2023 a goodly number of pilgrims made their way to Asbury from near and far expecting holy flash and froth, only to be disappointed, at least initially. That is until they tasted the sweet fruit of the calmer, gentler manner of worship in Wilmore. Asbury Seminary Old Testament Professor Lawson Stone speaks to this issue:

> A constant theme in all the revivals we've experienced here that led to transformation is a lack of emphasis on

manifestations, gifts, miracles, or sensationalism. It's confession, repentance, reconciliation, restitution, and renewed love. People try to get control of it and the sweet water just runs through their fingers.[13]

Physical healings are reported to have occurred in and out of Hughes Auditorium. Just as important, and more in evidence in February 2023, was "deep emotional healing and reconciliation," commented Thomas Lyons. "These manifestations of divine love are as dramatic as the opening of deaf ears."[14]

Testimonials of Transformation

Worship leaders in Hughes periodically held microphones for those who wanted to share what God was doing in their lives. Especially in the early days many students came forward to speak of their new or deeper life in Christ. Leaders requested that everyone "observe these ABCs: All glory to God alone; be brief; and be current."[15] Professor Nicholson notes:

> Testimonies have been moving and powerful. . . . Students have publicly confessed addictions to pornography, anger at God, bitterness of heart, despair as the result of difficult family situations, and so much more. For some of these students, I know their stories, and through the semesters I have seen their anxiety, depression, and deep wounds. Yet now they proclaim healing, joy, and a deep love of God like they have never before experienced. This is not manufactured emotionalism.[16]

Sometimes worship leaders followed a student's word of a specific deliverance with a call for others with a similar burden to stand. Prayers then followed for all those so afflicted, with fellow students gathered close around in support. One student who was among those who lingered after chapel on February 8 is a worship leader. Sarah Cawley, by her own account, came to Asbury angry and unsaved, and testified to her approaching graduation now freed from anger. Following Sarah's witness Pastor Zach Meerkreebs, who was holding the microphone, asked students struggling with anger issues to stand, and at least twelve rose. He then asked Sarah to pray for her fellow students dealing with anger.[17]

Dr. Sarah Baldwin and Chaplain Greg Haseloff became intentional in "building ministry time off of testimonies," as occurred in Pastor Meerkreebs's call for all present dealing with anger issues to receive community prayers of deliverance. Dr. Baldwin shared that those shepherding worship came to recognize four afflictions that were weighing students down and from which many found release: addictions, anxieties, "church hurt," and what she called "the spirit of death" (self-harm and thoughts of suicide). As an example, in a staccato-style listing of after-action bullet points, Dr. Baldwin was blunt: "So many high schoolers praying for relief from the bondage of pornography. Parents, step in! Take away phones, keep them out of bedrooms. Your children are DESPERATE!"[18]

By about the fourth day, Saturday, February 11, a pattern developed of ten to fifteen testimonies in the afternoon. Then in evening worship Dr. Baldwin or Chaplain Haseloff would ask two or three students to share about God's work in their lives.[19] Sunday morning, February 12, Pastor Meerkreebs asked if there were those who would share from the Psalms. For twenty or so minutes people stood to take turns reading a psalm—some in the back, some near the front, some from the balcony—orderly and devotionally without human direction. Board chair Larry Brown said it was one of the most beautiful moments of the awakening for him.[20]

Assistant professor of journalism Rich Manieri published the following account in the *Asbury Collegian*'s February 24 edition:

I know a young woman, Gracie, a talented student who, by her admission, turned her back on God. "Yeah, I know, I know," was her typical response to any attempt to reintroduce her to Jesus. Then, Feb. 8 happened, and as day turned into night and night turned back into day, Gracie sat in Hughes Auditorium and wept. At that moment, she surrendered her life to Jesus Christ. Then, Sunday night, this quiet young woman who makes barely a peep in class stood up—weeping again—and gave a testimony before an auditorium filled mostly with strangers. A few days later, she was baptized. She subsequently shared her testimony on national television. . . .

Gracie isn't preoccupied trying to describe what happened to her. She knows only that she had an encounter with Jesus. . . . It's all that really matters.[21]

While many students testified in Hughes Auditorium, others used the campus newspaper to do the same. In "When the Dust Settles," Anna Lowe paused to reflect:

I sit in the back row of the Hughes balcony. My legs are starting to ache from stiffly sitting in the same position for so long. . . . The light shifts with the sun through the yellow, artfully crafted, stained glass windows facing me.

"Our affection, our devotion, poured out on the feet of Jesus."

Over and over again this refrain repeats. . . . After my 1:00 p.m. class on Wednesday, I felt called to go to Hughes. Lately, my heart has been incredibly hardened. It was full of frustration due to so many situations in my life that I felt unheard and unvalued. . . . When I arrived at Hughes, my immediate inclination was to take photos and record what was happening through interviews, as my [Collegian] job typically requires. In my heart, I felt an outer nudge to be still. And so that's what I did. . . . All that mattered at that moment was our Creator.[22]

Collegian writer Sara Clark relates another testimony of deliverance:

On Sunday nights, it's fairly common to see a hundred or more students at the World Gospel Mission (WGM) student center. It's dedicated time for worship, fellowship, testimonies from missionaries across the globe—and some of the best home-cooked meals on campus. It was here on Feb. 5, the Sunday before the Holy Spirit fell on Hughes Auditorium, that freshman Brooke O'Carroll [recalled:] "God convicted my heart of a sin I had intentionally pushed into the back of my mind." . . .

O'Carroll described the experience as darkness being brought into the light . . .

When on Feb. 8, 2023, Wednesday's chapel continued, O'Carroll knew she had to go back to Hughes. . . .

"I stayed there six hours and just sat in the Lord's presence."

She didn't want to leave . . . God . . . helped her surrender idols like school and forgive those who had hurt her. She said she "felt the burden lift" as she truly surrendered everything to Jesus.

On the first Saturday of the revival, Director of [Asbury's] Christian Life Project Jeannie Banter felt prompted for people in attendance to pray over family hurt and families in general.

"Stand if your family is on your heart and we will pray over you," Banter said.

O'Carroll had stood up and received prayer on their behalf . . . [then] found herself kneeling on the altar. . . .

"When I returned to my seat there was a text that . . . [my family] got the last room in the Asbury Inn."

At the outpouring with them, she called the prayer time as a family "surreal."

"Sunday night I surrendered everything . . . every piece of my heart and asked for prayer for freedom from my past. I was freed and empty so God could use me."[23]

Carolina Trumpower, also in the *Collegian*, put her testimony of blessing and release succinctly:

One of the scariest and most healing moments for me during the revival was when I went to the altar. Confessing is terrifying, but there is beauty and freedom in repenting in front of a crowd. Sometimes the Holy Spirit speaks to us in a still, small voice, and other times, in an intense compulsion to be honest and vulnerable with those around you. There is peace in answering God's call and doing or saying what He is laying on your heart.[24]

As noted, worship leaders often called for prayers for those present in Hughes who had special needs or responsibilities, asking them to stand in place. On one occasion special prayers were offered for church lay leaders. A Wilmore resident, a devoted church worker, but unfamiliar with anything like a spontaneous Asbury revival, slowly stood along with others. At that moment a person he did not know put a hand on his shoulder and said, "I want to pray for your children and grandchildren." This gesture brought tears to the eyes of this lay leader who was touched by that "tie that binds our hearts in Christian love"—just like Asbury's Gen Zers.[25]

Worship in Summary

The spontaneous, Holy Spirit– and student-generated season of renewal that enveloped Asbury University and Asbury Seminary was characterized by a widely felt sense of the presence of the divine; simple praise choruses that were sometimes exuberant, sometimes contemplative; a sense of time standing still; an absence of celebrities; low-key, low-tech worship; an abundance of prayers of repentance, confession, and forgiveness at the altar, in the aisles, and in seats; and public testimonies. These two weeks were also bathed in prayer, Scripture reading, Communion on February 11 for approximately fifteen hundred worshippers, and proclamation of the Word by university and seminary administrators, faculty, and staff. When calls went out offering worshippers an opportunity to share Scripture passages of their choice, long lines formed. Following each reading the worship leader intoned, "The Word of God," with everyone in Hughes responding, "and we believe it."

As for the preaching, the names and titles of those sharing the Word were rarely announced. Pastor Bill Elliff reported: "One prognosticator on social media proclaimed that this [Asbury Outpouring] was not of God because there was no preaching. I smiled because there have been moments of preaching throughout and a 'regular' sermon every night."[26] Tim Beougher from Louisville's Southern Seminary and West Broadway Baptist Church appreciated the preaching he heard:

> I mentioned to my church recently that I haven't heard much talk among evangelicals in recent years about "dying to self." . . . I don't hear much about it anymore. This afternoon [at Asbury] there was teaching on dying to self that was followed by a directed prayer time asking God to help us do just that. The focus was clear: die to self and live for Christ and others. That is biblical.[27]

The very same point was explicit in Zach Meerkreebs's February 8 chapel message on the cusp of the spontaneous revival.

five

LEADERSHIP AND LOGISTICS
Coping with Blessing

"Administrators, campus ministry staff, and student leaders have been working overtime, sometimes on little sleep, trying to guard the [Asbury] movement's integrity and focus." So wrote Asbury Seminary Professor Craig Keener on February 16, 2023.[1] To their credit, members of the Asbury University cabinet take their faith seriously and are seasoned veterans in their particular fields of responsibility. For his part, President Kevin Brown, in his position just since 2019, has gained the equivalent of at least a decade's worth of experience shepherding the university through the uncharted territory of COVID-19 response. He has often remarked he was not given a playbook to manage that crisis. Nor was he given a playbook to superintend the spontaneous combustion of a spiritual awakening on Asbury's campus that social media transformed into a national and international phenomenon.[2] University retiree Jeanette Davis, who for many hours manned a check-in desk for volunteers, overheard someone remark that Asbury was building a plane while it was on the runway.[3]

The mutual respect and shared purpose of President Brown's administrative team, coupled with their modeling of servant leadership, goes a good way toward explaining how, at least in human terms, Asbury University was able to success-fully weather a perfect storm of spiritual blessing in February 2023. Not only the president and his cabinet, but staff, students, and a quickly assembled army of well over a thousand volunteers all gave generously of their time. Information Technology administrator Paul Dupree said he averaged four hours' sleep per night for two weeks, and some days he had to bike to campus because of unprecedented traffic congestion and police road-blocks. Vice President Mark Whitworth said he rarely got home before midnight: "I was running on fumes." Vice President Sarah Baldwin was having to make decisions "on the fly." Information Technology staffer Andy Miller, who has worked at Asbury for twelve years, was "blown away" by the worship, the camaraderie of everyone working together, and the careful, prayerful leader-ship of the administration. President Brown, in turn, "saw the utter best of our campus community—men and women who steadfastly redirected their effort and energy to maintain an orderly and hospitable environment. Radical humility. Radical generosity. Radical hospitality."[4] Nothing could better illustrate the point than a cabinet member and two faculty cleaning rest-rooms in the basement of Hughes.[5]

In a February 16 communiqué Brown acknowledged the exceptional gifts of service he was witnessing:

> I have . . . been deeply inspired by the incredible spirit of our Asbury staff, faculty, and students. I have seen men and women go far above and beyond in every way imag-inable to accommodate our visitors so they can encounter the Lord on our campus. I have seen faculty and staff work between classes to bring order, usher lines, pass out water, and pray with students. I have had students share their desire to make space for guests to experience what they have. **Never in my life will I forget this. Never in my life have I been so proud to say that I am a part of**

Asbury University. I write this with tears. The people
here are so special.[6]

During the pressure-packed first days of the revival, the
administration's first order of business was discerning how best to
serve as its host. President Brown shared with his leadership team:
"Something really historic and really unique is happening here.
This is going to outlive us. Well after we're dead, people are going
to be talking about this. Are we going to accommodate it?" The
answer was yes, but not, they hoped, at the expense of students.
When asked what was his toughest call during Asbury's spiritual
outpouring, his response was this: "Tension between fostering
something historic, visible, and powerful" and "recognizing my
responsibility . . . for our school's student-centric mission." The
administration's guiding principle was to somehow address the
needs of both students and pilgrims. It was no easy juggling act.

President Brown was particularly candid in his February 16
public communiqué:

> As an Asbury University leader, there is a tension I am
> trying to faithfully navigate at this time. On one hand, I
> humbly recognize we are experiencing a historic moment
> on our campus. Never in my life have I witnessed such
> manifest spiritual hunger—from our students to the
> nations—to humble ourselves and seek the Lord's face.
> Books could be (and will be) written recounting the
> incredible stories and experiences of inspiring humility,
> altar consecration, neighborly love, and life-changing
> commitments. When I walk into Hughes Auditorium I
> have a firsthand picture of the fruit of the Spirit.
>
> On the other hand, Asbury is a university. Our first
> commitment is to foster the minds and hearts of students
> who have been entrusted to us and who are central to our
> mission. We know the last week has been a disruption

to the continuity of their academic experience. Students have not only had to juggle various campus commitments (academic, athletic, extra-curricular, internship) with our various campus services, but also the throngs of people who have entered the dimensions of their space. For some, this has created a sense of being unsettled and even alienation from their campus community.[7]

Southern Seminary's Professor Tim Beougher, with experience having been one of those shepherding Wheaton College's 1995 spontaneous revival, credited Asbury's leadership for "a magnificent job of balancing freedom and order. . . . I know the incredible challenges of trying to maintain that balance."[8] Kenny Rager, Kentucky Baptist Convention church evangelism strategist, was in Hughes Auditorium Saturday night, February 11:

Everything pointed to God and was very Christ-centered. . . .

It wasn't a stifling or restricting kind of order because there was also a freedom for people to testify, sing, or pray. . . .

I was encouraged to see the staff shepherding the revival movement. They are keeping order, giving instructions and announcements but still encouraging the freedom of the spirit.[9]

The decision not to highlight nor even introduce worship teams and speakers was made in tandem with the decision to focus all attention on Christ. Arkansas Pastor Bill Elliff was pleased to note that "The wise pastors on Asbury's staff who are gently shepherding this movement keep reminding us that there are no superstars and that no one is to be exalted except Jesus. They have encouraged us to get lower and lower and lower under Him, exalting Him higher and higher."[10]

Dr. Steve Seamands, a student participant in the 1970 Asbury Revival and a retired Asbury Seminary professor, made the same point. With Jesus of the Incarnation in mind, he said, "God can go low." It is a "downward direction" that is the example to follow. John the Baptist said he had to decrease so Christ could increase (see John 3:30). "We just don't want to be little enough." Then Dr. Seamands called to mind the oft-quoted 2 Chronicles 7:14 passage: "If my people, who are called by my name, will *humble* themselves . . ."[11] J. D. Walt of Seedbed put it simply: "Jesus is the only celebrity here." That was the case, he believed, because:

> No one even remotely considers the names of anyone in leadership here. They are not unseasoned, just unknown . . . and they will to stay that way. Incredible humility characterizes this whole move. The leadership at Asbury University has been an extraordinary servant to Jesus in this. Kevin Brown, the president, is its chief champion.[12]

Dr. Timothy Tennent noted that the concept of "radical humility . . . came forth independently from numerous people" and from the grassroots up. It was taken up as a prevailing posture of servanthood by staff and volunteers on both sides of Lexington Avenue.[13]

It could be a bit mystifying for visitors from off campus. When a seminary professor from Lexington asked who was in charge, she was told, "No one is."[14] The modern world—and too many in the Christian world—just "do not get" servant leadership. Provost Sherry Powers recalled standing in the back of Hughes with the president when someone came up to him and asked how he was going to manage what was happening. His response: "My goal is to stay out of the way of the Holy Spirit."[15] Wednesday night, February 22, I was ushering in Hughes when I observed a dressed-down Dr. Brown make his way from the very back seats of Hughes to the front, and with the altar full, he quietly knelt in prayer along with others kneeling before the front row of seats. Traditionally, it is where faculty have sat during thrice-weekly chapel services.

A corollary to Asbury leadership's decision to focus on Christ was the decision to focus on students and their spiritual grounding through the ongoing worship in Hughes Auditorium. That the administration was unable after the first few days to maintain a completely student-oriented focus to the revival was a consequence of social media and the resulting flood of people pouring into a limited-capacity campus and a two-traffic-light Wilmore. *Collegian* editor Alexandra Presta said, "Someone posted a TikTok video [and] it blew up from there."[16] It was "a holy calm" in the beginning, according to Professor David Swartz. "But then the world came."[17] The question for Vice President for Business Affairs Glenn Hamilton was how to accommodate "50,000 of your new best friends."[18] For Asbury Seminary Professor Jason Vickers, it felt like the renewal was "being usurped by pilgrims."[19]

Still, administrators did what they could. To protect students who were sometimes giving very personal public confessions, an early call was made not to livestream Hughes worship and to discourage smartphone recordings by visitors. Those decisions were well-intentioned, but proved impossible to enforce.[20] It was not until February 19, twelve days in, that the administration chose to livestream worship in Hughes, and then just to accommodate the thousands of pilgrims who had little chance at a seat in a fifteen-hundred-seat auditorium. "In our world of 24/7 access," marveled Northern Seminary Professor Thomas Lyons, "it is almost unheard of for an event to *not* try to increase exposure through media."[21] As more and more pilgrims began filling Hughes, it was decided to rope off front rows for Asbury students. As Asbury Seminary President Tennent explained, university leaders "wisely reserved the central, front section of the chapel for the students themselves, since this is *their* space and God chose to begin this work among *them*."[22]

As Hughes increasingly turned into a destination for pilgrims and as students felt less at home there, university leaders considered additional measures. The administration was thankful for the numerous Asbury Seminary and local church overflow venues since it could not utilize its Luce Center basketball court because of the ongoing intercollegiate athletics schedule and limited parking. The auditorium in the Shaw Collaborative Learning Center also came up for consideration, but ongoing classes and security concerns in this newly opened facility nixed it as an overflow venue. However, this same auditorium was converted temporarily into an alternative students-only worship space with its own Hughes simulcast, snacks, and beverages.[23]

While Provost Powers shared there was "total consensus to continue classes," faculty did make accommodations with assignments, and the second weekend (February 17–19) "a lot of faculty opened their homes to students" who were stressed out by the press of humanity on campus.[24] Still, the crowds got to students, as Communications Professor Heather Hornbeak noted in her journal:

> I had one student on Day 5 walking to her 11:00 course crying. She's a solid upper classman so I knew something was really wrong when I saw her upset. She had come from chapel, and all students were surprised to be greeted by a sea of visitors waiting at the front doors. . . . It was too much for them. . . . Many made comments about feeling pressured to "take care of the adults" while also feeling invaded by them. One group of students coming into class told the story of one lady in line shouting, "Oh look, there they are! They are all going to class!" while taking photos of them as if they were celebrities.[25]

Collegian editor Alexandra Presta has a gift for cogent description and critique:

> It can be exciting to have so many honored guests here. . . . However, we're asking you to respect us, too.
>
> Our campus can be intriguing. The [Miller] communications building has all kinds of cool artifacts. The pristine Walt and Rowena Shaw Collaborative Learning Center's bright lights act almost like a beckoning to come and explore. Other structures hold so much nostalgia and history.
>
> But if that's why you are coming to Asbury, you have come for the wrong reasons. Our students are not coming to Hughes to worship to help influencers, news stations, and ordinary people increase their social media subscriptions, likes and follows. Our dorms are not meant to be wandered. . . .
>
> Classes are still occurring . . . However, our focus has been deterred; our safety is becoming at risk. . . .
>
> We love God and what He is doing. But love is respectful. It is patient and kind, as 1 Corinthians 13 says.[26]

As a gospel choir member put it: "We want our home back."[27]

Dr. Brown's February 14 and 16 communiqués spoke to this priority:

> As president, I can assure you I am working with other key leaders to intentionally and faithfully steward our students in a manner that maintains continuity and creates space for their university experience as well as this generous outpouring of God's Spirit on our campus.[28]

> While I remain profoundly grateful that staff, faculty, and students get to be a part of God's unique and powerful work on our campus, I want to be mindful

of my mandate as a fiduciary of Asbury's resources and student-centric mission.[29]

Because of concern for students' educational as well as spiritual welfare, and because of an overtaxed staff and an overwhelmed Wilmore, President Brown, on February 16, announced the administration's decision to give benediction to public services on campus in one week's time, to end February 23. It was one of the most (if not the most) difficult decisions he had to make in February 2023.[30]

When asked if he was "stopping this outpouring of God's Spirit," he responded: "We cannot stop something we did not start." The revival's spreading to other campuses underscored that point.[31] CBN—and even some attention-minded champions of revival—criticized the university for "quenching the Spirit."[32] But the fact was it became physically impossible to continue. The Asbury institutions and tiny Wilmore, as well, simply were not designed to accommodate tens of thousands of unexpected visitors, even when the vast majority were well-behaved and peaceable. Mayor Harold Rainwater itemized the issues confronting the city as visitors continued to max out facilities: difficult access to groceries, gas, and laundromat; Wilmore's few restaurants running out of food; not enough restrooms; no place to park; concern for open roadways for fire, police, and emergency vehicles; utter exhaustion of city and business workers.[33] The same concerns were stressing the university and seminary as well.

Professor Hornbeak saw that "stopping the revival" was a trending theme on social media, which she sought to address online:

> I described the sheer weight of cleaning the sanctuary with the understaffed custodial team and wanting the people who made it here to be safe and taken care of. Asbury couldn't host this many people well forever. It was unsustainable and needed to spread. Looking back, I

wish I had mentioned our dedication to our students and deep respect for our leadership shepherding us through what to do next.[34]

The university understood that it had a contractual obligation to provide students with a full spring semester of academic instruction. Certainly, February 2023 would forever be a spiritual touchstone for the Asbury community. Still, the everyday and the routine are not to be despised, as Brother Lawrence put it so humbly, yet eloquently, in *The Practice of the Presence of God*. While Asbury's ethos is to hold and cherish seasons of spiritual refreshing, they are not thought to be to the exclusion of its existence as an educational institution. On a personal level the body needs rest as well as endeavor, and the human spirit, in company with spiritual exaltation, needs time to ponder things of the heart. Asbury's administration rightly recognized its dual calling to shepherd an unanticipated spiritual outpouring, but not to the neglect of its academic reason for being.

six

SHEPHERDING THE UNEXPECTED

Decision-Making "Just in Time"

Throughout sixteen days, Asbury's cabinet had to make critical decisions—and a lot of them and with no time to spare. A handful of administrators and key staff met with President Brown, often in a storage room behind the platform in Hughes Auditorium. Advancement and Christian Life staffer Jeannie Banter recalled the space was so cramped half of those present stood and half sat on the floor. Then they shifted to 214 Reasoner Hall connected to Hughes, which came to be dubbed the "Command Center."[1] As days passed, meetings were "all over the place," in the words of Vice President for Business Affairs Glenn Hamilton—some still in the "Command Center" classroom in Reasoner Hall, some in the Hager Administration Building former board room, some in the first-floor "Search Studio" and the second-floor conference room in the new Shaw Collaborative Learning Center, some in Dr. Tennent's office at the seminary.[2]

Mark Whitworth, vice president for athletics and university communications, recalled: "We began getting reports from people seeing stuff on social media about people who were coming, not just from our region, but pretty significant distances. . . . But the focus was on practical things. Like, does the worship team need to rest, and do we have enough prayer support at the altar?"[3]

Questions and decisions in response came in rapid succession. That first night of February 8, would they keep Hughes open? Yes, as long as students remained to pray and praise, which ended up being through the night. Then in following days, should student musicians and speakers be identified by name? No. What about counselors for the growing press of students at the altar? Beyond Asbury faculty and staff, it was decided to recruit trusted community pastors and laity and others with ties to the university who were given lanyards for their ready identification as counselors.

Should overhead screens be used to provide lyrics? The decision was no, for fear worship might become too scripted. Should filming by visitors be allowed? At first, as noted, the answer was no, then later the decision was university-produced live streaming. What about the prayer requests that began pouring in? Asbury IT set up an email account: prayer@asbury.edu.[4]

What about classes? Would they be canceled? No. Unlike in 1970, the decision was for instruction to continue, a course Asbury Seminary followed as well. University Provost Sherry Powers noted that with burgeoning numbers of visitors on campus, "classes were a safe place" and a familiar setting where "faculty connected faith and learning."[5] For students living in an anxious age, classrooms became sanctuaries on a campus that was rapidly filling with mostly well-meaning, but still mostly unknown pilgrims. Seminary President Tennent also favored continuing classes:

> It is not because we are in "business as usual" mode. Far from it. There is talk of little else in every chapel, in every classroom, in every hallway conversation, and, I suspect, in every home and apartment in the community. . . . We all love mountaintop experiences, but we also know that they must be lived out in all the normal rhythms of life.[6]

At the same time, academic allowances had to be made. They ranged from revised syllabi to postponed deadlines to ad hoc tutorials to compensate for classes missed in favor of worship in Hughes Auditorium.

None of Asbury's administrators had ever been a part of anything like what was unfolding before their eyes—an unexpected spiritual awakening sparked by a few dozen students that literally brought the world to Wilmore, including sojourners from at least forty states and forty countries. What do you do when the world lands on your doorstep with no prior notice? Well, the Bible says you welcome the stranger, and Asbury and Wilmore did. Scripture is very clear on this point: "Do not neglect to show hospitality to strangers, for thereby some have entertained angels unawares" (Heb. 13:2 ESV); "Show hospitality to one another without grumbling" (1 Peter 4:9 ESV).

The situation called for rapid-fire decision-making under pressures that at some points felt like controlled chaos. Paul Dupree, director of IT, called it "seat of the pants" management. Glen Hamilton called it "just in time."[7] Multiple administrators used the word "fluid" to describe the ever-changing worship and demographic landscape. Sarah Baldwin gave her Facebook followers a sense of the sixteen days of scrambling behind the scenes:

> Everyone mobilized and supported 24-hour infrastructure for crowds on a dime. At some point . . . we saw the crowds were picking up and we started planning an evening event for what would be 3,000 in literally under an hour—pivot, adapt, move, change, stretch, grow. . . . The infrastructure of it all has been a text thread. I just love this. For all my spreadsheets, organizational plans for all the administrative work we do at AU, when it comes down to it, we have had a text thread keeping us in step with each other. Literally minute by minute.[8]

When texting could no longer accommodate everyone who needed to be in the loop, Paul Dupree switched everyone to greater capacity WhatsApp. He said it was "like a war of logistics in the best sense."[9] Baldwin captured the mile-a-minute climate of those days:

> I want to remember the WhatsApp thread, 101 notifications at a time, "Water needed in Estes!" "Is there a prayer volunteer for out in the line?" "Portapotties overflowing!" "10 people gave their hearts to Jesus here!" "The huge JESUS flag needs to come down!" "What's that ambulance for?" "It's 30 degrees out here. Heaters are on the way." "The Sal Army showed up. Thank you, Jesus!"[10]

Mark Whitworth, with decades of experience with Southeastern Conference sports administration under his belt, described a scene completely different from any of his SEC experiences: "The first few days it was altar mode; then for me it was media mode; then it was management mode." In that third stage, with thousands on campus unable to access fifteen-hundred-seat Hughes, he proposed an outdoor semicircle simulcast venue, which came to pass in just hours. Unlike his SEC year to year-and-a-half event planning cycles, it was hour-by-hour provisioning, "like Jesus and the loaves and fishes," not the only administrator to call to mind Jesus's "supply chain" miracle by the seashore.[11]

Glenn Hamilton, with decades of administrative experience, had seen "nothing like this." He continued: "I like structure. That was thrown out the window. It was so fluid. Who is available now? I literally laugh when people ask about our planning. There was no plan!" What was his biggest challenge? "It was the speed of decision-making in relation to the crowds." How did he handle it? "We took care of each other. It was a unique bonding experience." Surprisingly, Hamilton recalled no one was "cranky or mean" despite the exhaustion. Thinking back on February 2023 and getting emotional, he is certain, "I will be in awe for the rest of my life."[12] For Sarah Baldwin it was the same: "I have felt the prayers of hundreds, sustaining and supporting. So much encouragement and kindness. Thank you. I will remember these days for the rest of my life and how much love and grace came to us. It's all a gift. My faith is encouraged. Thank you."[13]

Unanticipated Expenses—and Unanticipated Donations

President Brown and Dr. Mark Troyer, vice president for advancement, realized the spiritual awakening would affect the institution's finances. Nevertheless, they decided at the outset to suspend normal fundraising activities. When the revival broke out, President Brown canceled a flight to Florida, postponing scheduled alumni gatherings. Dr. Troyer, already in Florida, cut short his itinerary, including visits with donors. He also set aside the annual winter on-campus fundraising phonathon. At the same time, Dr. Troyer and Glenn Hamilton had to keep in mind mounting, unanticipated expenses ranging from increased campus security to purchases of pallets of bottled water to the rental of thirty-six portable toilets for the unexpected thousands of visitors.

The administration's counterintuitive decision was to take up no offerings and forego normal advancement solicitations. Why? Dr. Troyer specifically had in mind the warning found in Philippians 1:15 and 17: "Some preach Christ out of envy and rivalry . . . out of selfish ambition, not sincerely." According to one advancement team member: "None of us felt right about fund raising during a revival." The university administration wanted no possibility that anyone would think Asbury was profiting off of revival.[14]

That stance is in contrast to the cable channel that requires a donation before one can view its Asbury Revival documentary. Speaking of commercialization, Amazon is now selling an unauthorized "Asbury Revival 2023 Worship Throw Pillow" and an "Asbury Revival 2023 Praise and Worship Pullover Hoodie," in one's choice of colors, no less. Asbury's season of renewal enjoyed many expressions of selflessness. Would that a season of renewal, with so many expressions of selflessness in holding a work of God gently, could be spared being sullied by such crass profiteering.

Though unplanned expenses soared well into six figures, unanticipated and unsolicited donations miraculously matched the outflow. Advancement staffer Jeannie Banter remembered weeping when she received financial statements confirming funds were coming in to cover unbudgeted expenses. The way this happened continually amazed Dr. Troyer. One day he was walking among hundreds of visitors on the campus semicircle lawn, with nothing to designate him as official other than an Asbury logo on his pullover. Someone he did not know walked up to him and asked if he could accept a donation for the university. Dr. Troyer said yes, at which point he was given a check for twenty thousand dollars from a church in Florida that had anticipated that Asbury would need extra help with so many unexpected worshippers.[15] In the same spirit someone from Alabama contacted Mayor Harold Rainwater to tell him a check was on the way for one thousand dollars for city expenses. The mayor had never met the man.[16]

Protecting the Revival from Attention Seekers

Some of the most difficult decisions centered on the level of participation that would be permitted by worshippers new to Asbury. University cabinet members safeguarded the worship platform as well as the main floor and balcony seating.[17] Sarah Baldwin and Greg Haseloff vetted testimonies, and as a precaution, held on to the microphone. Their mantra was "Don't let go"—in order to preserve Christ-centered worship.[18]

Dr. Baldwin related that Saturday and Sunday, February 11 and 12, "We were asked all day long, 'Can I give a word? Give a word? Give word?' 'Well, tell us your word first.'"[19] Staff shepherding of worship was handled with sensitivity and charity, but also with discernment and caution. Well-known, award-winning Christian musicians and a number of denominational leaders headed to Wilmore, but accepted the university's decision to offer them seating but not a microphone.[20]

The concern of Dr. Baldwin and other worship leaders for what took place on the platform of Hughes was completely justified. Laura Levens, the Baptist seminary professor from Lexington, recognized that Asbury's leaders had to "safeguard the revival from people who want to co-opt the stage."[21] Robert Kanary, author of *Spontaneous Revivals: Asbury College 1905–2006*, understood that "Those who want a name for themselves often hijack movements that God initiates among the lowly. . . . Some may come for hype or to seek attention for themselves."[22] Arkansas Pastor Elliff was an eyewitness to preventive actions by Asbury staff: "I have personally watched them stop a person or two who may have tried to hijack the meeting."[23]

For much of the time student worship teams led praise choruses in a spirit that could best be described as gentle, soulful, even prayerful. In contrast, there were periods of exuberant, even boisterous praise, especially among visitors new to Asbury, so much so that worship leaders had to announce no more jumping in place in the balcony—which is nearly one hundred years old.

Quite a few who traveled to Wilmore to experience Asbury's spiritual outpouring appeared to have more ecstatic worship in mind. Asbury University history professor David Swartz saw firsthand how this could play out. Volunteering before and after his classes, he moved cases of water, ushered, checked bags, and on occasion guarded Hughes's designated entrance for the public, jokingly referring to himself as Asbury's part-time "Mennonite bouncer." If that sounds like hyperbole, consider that this Christian pacifist now has quite a collection of knives retrieved from pilgrim backpacks, only a portion of which fit the innocent pocketknife description. (Most worshippers never returned to Dr. Swartz to pick up their hardware!) This history professor observed his fair share of sojourners to Asbury arriving with anticipation of a high decibel, high-tech, high-powered worship experience, only to be let down, more often than not, by praise to the Lord closer in temperament to peace and quiet. Some, Swartz noticed, accommodated themselves to the spirit of the place and even came to appreciate the relatively subdued tenor of worship. But others tried to vocally energize congregants to satisfy their own definition of praise to the Lord, shouting and jumping in place.[24]

From Asbury's perspective, much more problematic than those bent on a charismatic style of worship were view-counting religion bloggers and ministry personalities intent on increased publicity for their brand and their social media platforms, those whom J. D. Walt referred to as revival "storm chasers." As Asbury University past president David Gyertson consoled President Brown, "The gospel light sometimes attracts some pretty strange bugs."[25] Asbury Seminary Old Testament Professor Lawson Stone is at no loss for words in his colorful Facebook post skewering unhealthy revival hangers on:

> Every move of the Spirit will also attract crazies, semi-heretics, sectarians, legalists, and populists wanting to run to the front and claim they are leading it. At the margins are all the nit pickers and nay-sayers, the ones starting sentences with "We'll know it's REALLY revival when . . ." We've also got a guy riding in the back of a pickup truck with a bullhorn. . . . He sounds belligerent even as he quotes scriptures about God's love.

This outpouring has been characteristically "Jesus!" oriented. Not Jesus and politics. . . . [Some] will try to use Jesus to leverage a focus on something else. They'll drop in a word about some pet conspiracy theory or some ideological hobby horse, and they will actually USE Jesus to get you fired up about their cause. It's subtle but watch for it. Many of the freelance preachers in town super-ficially preach the gospel, but you can tell they want to move you to [politics]. . . . Have fresh batteries in your "Latent Paranoia Detector" and make sure it's turned on and active! This is going to be a great week to practice spiritual and theological discernment! . . .

For two weeks, we were simply gathered around Jesus. And now, out in the lawns, circles of people gathered around preachers. One circle around this preacher, another circle around that preacher. For some reason this gives me a heart ache. I know preaching is vital to the health of the church, and these probably aren't bad preachers, but it just looks so . . . about THEM. Am I wrong? . . . There are always people who want to be present during a time like this, and preachers, well, they like to preach! They want to be active in it. Lesser souls want to be able to say, "I preached at the Asbury outpouring of 2023."[26]

Like party crashers, revival crashers are all about attention, and too often, harm. Todd Bentley is a Canadian-born charis-matic dis-fellowshipped by his denomination in 2020 following a pastors' investigation that documented a "steady pattern of immoral conduct."[27] The Asbury administration was forewarned that he had announced falsely that he had been invited to lead worship at Asbury and had told his Twitter followers, "I'm going." He did, but once identified in Hughes, he was gently escorted off the prem-ises. Mark Whitworth, no stranger to outsized personalities in the SEC sports world, had the assignment of protecting worshippers from whatever Bentley might attempt, once he was spotted in the auditorium. With university communications as part of his portfolio, Whitworth "communicated" to Bentley, quietly but firmly, that he would have to leave because he had misrepresented his involvement with the revival. Asbury's VP was able to pray with Bentley, who then, somewhat surprisingly, exited Hughes without incident. Whitworth considered this peaceful resolution one of the many miracles of the Asbury Outpouring.[28] Also heading for Wilmore—but disallowed—was Greg Locke, shrill and dangerously outspoken in support of his political opinions. These were the types of distractions Asbury definitely did not want.[29]

Above all else, Asbury's leaders sought to protect the revival's spirit of unity, love, and forbearance that was much in evidence across generational, denominational, and racial lines. To that end, the university did everything in its power to steer worship and visitors away from any manifestations of toxic American political divisions and culture wars. One worshipper brought into Hughes a shofar, the ram's horn historically associated with Judaism, but of late also associated with Christian nationalism. With an affinity for decorum and an aversion to political posturing, a university staffer ushered the ram horn–blower out of the auditorium. Other Christian nationalists conflating professions of faith and patriotism were not permitted to bring flags into Hughes Auditorium. "This is about Jesus, not America," wrote Northern Seminary Professor Thomas Lyons.[30]

More famously, Tucker Carlson, formerly of Fox News, planned a trip to Asbury, but the administration managed to dissuade him from coming. He not only complied but publicly complimented the university for turning down the publicity. He settled for a charitable, on-air interview with Asbury student body president Alison Prefater, who acquitted herself well on air.[31]

Time and time again, Asbury's season of spiritual renewal was protected from any major distraction or disturbance in ways that seemed impossible to explain in human terms.

seven

SECURITY AND SAFETY
"For What Could Have Happened, It Just Didn't"

Student Anxieties over the Flood of Visitors

The Asbury Outpouring may have been the first spontaneous revival instantaneously made known across the US and the globe through social media. Accounts of Gen Z students earnestly seeking the Lord day after day and through the night proved immensely attractive to a spiritually hungry nation and world. The resulting thousands upon thousands pouring into Wilmore ended any semblance of serenity in the normally peaceful village. Rather quickly it also altered the composition of worshippers in Hughes from mostly Asbury students to mostly visitors. Just a few days into the revival one astute observer from Lexington recognized that "the campus had turned into a host for others . . . and the students now live in the liminal space of being both audience and host in this revival."[1] Even students who enthusiastically welcomed the revival still found so many unexpected visitors disconcerting. Wrote one:

> Asbury is a small campus where, to some extent, you
> practically know every face here on campus. So going

from that to seeing thousands of strangers on your campus is overwhelming. A couple weeks ago, I would have had no problem walking all the way across campus at 11:00 p.m. to pick up a textbook from a friend, but now I have to be cautious about doing that because there's a bunch of strangers.[2]

Dr. David Hay, assistant vice president for campus safety, who understood student concerns, recalled one incident in Glide-Crawford Dormitory, home to hundreds of women. By this point the line to enter Hughes stretched the length of the front campus to encircle Glide-Crawford on three sides. Young women felt surrounded, especially as visitors began to inhabit the front porch and even photograph them unawares. With "all these unknown people" very close at hand, residents became hypersensitive to the point that a call came in to campus safety: "unauthorized male in Glide-Crawford." Fortunately, it was a false alarm: some students were frightened by a physical plant worker they did not recognize, even though he was in uniform with identification.[3]

Very early on the university administration took multiple steps to allay such anxieties. Provost Sherry Powers, for one, called February 2023 both "the greatest experience and the greatest challenge of my professional life," with "the most difficult decisions," none more pressing than her "great concern for student safety." Over her career in higher education, she called to mind "thirty years of active shooter training," and prayed Asbury would be spared the trauma of gun violence on its campus.[4]

On one occasion board chair Larry Brown noticed a somewhat agitated young man walking the aisles in Hughes Auditorium in a winter coat. It struck Brown as odd that it was buttoned up and that he kept rubbing thumbs and index fingers together in an odd manner. At one point this person slipped onto the platform where a worship leader met him at the top of the steps. A conversation ensued, at which point he left the stage. Brown stood by him for twenty or thirty minutes, attempting to engage in conversation. He was largely uncommunicative, but it did turn out he was an Asbury student. The platform worship leader later shared with Brown that the same day this student underwent a dramatic spiritual transformation, one that was very evident immediately and on campus afterward: "He was a completely different person." As it turned out, Brown had been observing a student under profound conviction, rather than someone bent on mayhem. But given the increasing number of school shootings, Asbury had to be careful.

On another occasion, a worship leader had an anxious moment as a couple from Chile told of selling their car to pay for flights to Asbury. Someone in the balcony suddenly gave a loud shout and threw something on the platform. To some it sounded like a gunshot. To everyone's relief it was not gunfire but just money being thrown onto the platform to help the Chileans return home.[5]

A Welcome Police Presence

To augment public safety and security, the administration welcomed protection provided by not only Wilmore police, but R. J. Corman Railroad Group security guards and a host of Bluegrass police departments including Nicholasville, Jessamine County, Lancaster, Garrard County, Danville, Boyle County, Versailles, Woodford County, Mercer County, and the University of Kentucky, for a total of ninety police officers during February 8–23. It helped that campus safety's David Hay is a former member of the Kentucky State Patrol, with longstanding ties with area police departments.[6]

Students were happy to have the officers on campus. A Danville policeman reported that he had been prayed over by Asbury students, which likely was not a lone instance. According to Dr. Hay, police felt very welcomed and appreciated on Asbury's campus, "not the day-to-day norm" in 2023 America. "It gave the university a good reputation."[7]

During the revival's peak second weekend, February 17–19, even Kentucky State Patrol did its part on US 68, diverting traffic from overloaded Route 29 to a somewhat less-congested Route 1268 into Wilmore. At the intersection a temporary road sign flashed "Revival at capacity," flash, "See livestreaming," flash, "Asbury.edu/outpouring."[8]

Dr. Hay was also in contact with North Carolina–based Samaritan's Purse, which contracted for and paid for six hundred hours for fifteen security guards to patrol the campus as visitors were wandering into classroom buildings and even dorms.[9] Hughes Auditorium proved an unusual security challenge because its connections with Reasoner Hall and Morrison Hall added up to a grand total of thirteen entrances. After just a few days a combination of police officers and volunteers manned each of these doors to secure the premises. In addition, the city of Wilmore moved its police dispatch to a conference room on the ground floor of Reasoner Hall, a space that eventually also accommodated a paramedic team (Alpha Medical) and a 911 operator.[10]

Even before the Michigan State University shooting on February 13, which left four dead and five wounded, the university cabinet and campus safety were implementing additional measures to keep worshippers safe. Many volunteers walked the line of visitors waiting for entrance to Hughes, passing out water, praying with people, and in the case of members of twelve Billy Graham Evangelistic Association volunteer teams, conducting unobtrusive but needful security reconnaissance. About the same time as the Michigan State tragedy, Asbury began bag checks for visitors entering Hughes Auditorium. The result was a collection of multiple boxes of impounded knives and canisters of pepper spray.[11] Across the street at a seminary overflow venue, President Tennent recalled one worshipper who unsuccessfully sought entrance with a handgun. Remarkably, over and over again reports were that pilgrims to Wilmore took bag checks and even the incredibly long lines in a charitable spirit.[12]

Handling Crowd Control Gently but Firmly

Accommodating ever-expanding numbers of sojourners stretched the university to the limit. Inside Hughes early days of standing room only and jumping in the balcony to music had to give way to safer worship.[13] Dr. Tennent shared that hosting renowned British theologian N. T. Wright a month before the outpouring, with multiple addresses at the seminary and one in Hughes Auditorium, gave some practice in dealing with larger-than-average numbers.[14] But as it turned out, attendance in those meetings paled before the flood of February's pilgrims. Early on, Mark Whitworth witnessed three hundred to four hundred people on the steps leading up to the front entrance of Hughes. With many years of experience with crowd control at SEC sports tournaments, he knew that scene was a disaster waiting to happen. One firecracker, much less a gun, or even a bullhorn blast, could have triggered a panic with potentially deadly consequences. On site, fortuitously, was Sam White, owner of Lexington's MSI events management company and father of an Asbury University student. He told Whitworth what he already knew: "You all aren't ready." On Asbury's behalf, on the spot White contacted a Lexington vendor with a supply of portable crowd fencing. Miraculously, in two hours Whitworth was in possession of four hundred to five hundred feet of this same fencing for the front of Hughes that moved people back a safe distance from the entrance.[15]

The Semicircle Lawn—Awash with Humanity

And then what to do with the line of pilgrims waiting to enter Hughes? It had to be directed and redirected as it kept growing and growing by the hour. Jeff Stryker, a university board member and owner of two popular Chick-fil-A franchises in Lexington, knew what crowd control needed to look like. He gave counsel on how to manage the queuing in line, moving it away from North Lexington Avenue, at least for the length of the safer semicircle's Macklem Drive.[16]

Then what about the semicircle lawn itself, which became the default venue for several thousand pilgrims intent upon worship? Just as prayer cells, support groups, and "mini-congregations" blossomed in the lines, the same instantaneous fellowships of spiritually hungry formed on the lawn in front of Hughes, Morrison Hall, Hager Administration Building, and Glide-Crawford Dormitory. As Professor Craig Keener remembered: "Believers who had never met before and would never meet again in this life experienced a common heart," both in Hughes and "outside . . . as many of those crowded on the lawn . . . worshipped and prayed together. Some Korean friends from another evangelical seminary came to visit, and we worshipped together on the lawn before moving to one of the overflow destinations."[17]

As entrance to Hughes became harder to come by, Paul Dupree and his IT staff scrambled to reproduce the indoor worship out of doors. Within the first week, they set up speakers, which allowed those on the semicircle lawn to at least hear the indoor worship. But as the crowds continued to swell, quite a few pilgrims were beyond the range of hearing. Next, Dupree and company set up a screen and transmitted a simulcast of Hughes worship to additional sojourners, with hundreds of folding chairs provided by Jeff Stryker and Glenn Hamilton. Then as storms rolled in on Thursday, February 16, the screen and speakers had to come down before a deluge of just over two inches of rain.[18] Flexible throughout, Asbury's IT staff took advantage of clear weather on the second weekend of the outpouring, February 18–19, to erect two simulcast screens. As Mark Whitworth put it, for thousands of worshippers "the lawn was an extension of Hughes."[19] Worship inside Hughes was frequently described as low-tech, and it was. But the extension of worship out of doors with no prior planning was no mean feat, all the more remarkable for having been produced "just in time."[20] Thanks to Asbury University staff adaptability and fortitude, Asbury Seminary Old Testament Professor Lawson Stone could write on Facebook: "For those coming, don't worry about not getting into Hughes. The semicircle is about as saturated with the Spirit as any place I've ever been."[21]

A Chronology of Campus Safety

Campus safety's David Hay was particularly well-positioned to appreciate the enormity of the security challenge posed by the influx of an estimated fifty thousand to seventy thousand people into Wilmore—and that without forewarning. Find below a portion of his memorable account of campus security, centered on beyond-exhaustion efforts to protect life and limb in February 2023:

- Wednesday, February 8: In the afternoon he observes students worshipping in Hughes. "It's pretty amazing." He marvels at the "overwhelming sense of peace in Hughes."
- Thursday February 9: With just our full-time and several part-time campus safety personnel, "We're trying to figure this out . . . We had no idea. . . . We don't have the staff to staff it." About 10:00 p.m. that night Dr. Hay receives a call from the night guard. "There are a thousand people here!"
- Friday, February 10: "We're beyond capacity." Dr. Hay thinks through "emergency management issues." He asks Wilmore police for help, and they give it. He is diagnosed with COVID: "All of a sudden I am out."

- Saturday, February 11: Two Wilmore police are on campus, with one on duty overnight. The fire marshal calls with his concerns. From home Dr. Hay recruits dozens of area police for overtime help. "It is expensive, but we have to have them." "I gave up on parking early on. It was beyond control."
- Sunday, February 12: An estimated three thousand worship in Hughes and overflow venues.
- Monday, February 13: The Michigan State shooting reinforces concerns for public safety, with thousands of unknown people in town. "Parents are calling. . . . Oh my gosh. Ninety-nine percent are here for the right reasons, but we are a target. I like to be trusting, but my job requires me not to be."
- Tuesday, February 14: Dr. Hay is back on campus after his COVID quarantine. President Kevin Brown is thankful for the outpouring but acknowledges that "the influx of visitors" is causing "a degree of unsettledness among our students."
- Wednesday, February 15: The 11:00 a.m. Asbury Seminary chapel service is over capacity.
- Thursday, February 16: President Kevin Brown announces that worship for the public will continue through February 19, with services for youth 16–25 through February 23. Dr. Hay wonders how his staff can hold up that long. They have been averaging 15- to 16-hour days for nine days. The beginning of the closure of Hughes from 2:00 a.m. to 8:00 a.m. gives some relief. It is a cold, rainy day. "We want to be hospitable—but standing in the rain for hours?" The question is how to accommodate so many.
- Friday, February 17: Clear weather and two simulcast screens on the semicircle are a help, but the high temperature is only 46°.[22]

The Asbury institutions and the city of Wilmore managed to avoid any serious incident or emergency, remarkable considering the crowds: no physical altercations, no arrests, no fatalities, and no serious injuries or car accidents.[23] If there had been serious trouble, it most likely would have been on Saturday, February 18. That was the day university safety director Hay called "the surge," with what he estimated were thirty thousand pilgrims in town that weekend and anywhere from seven thousand to twenty thousand visitors in Wilmore in twenty-four hours, more than doubling or tripling the village's head count. Dr. Hay said the semicircle was so "thick" with people it was barely possible to walk through them. "We're beyond our wildest dream. You could hardly move. Police were on North Lexington Avenue trying to keep people from getting hit by cars. We had a public safety crisis on our hands. There was no way to get a fire truck through."[24]

In addition to worship in Hughes and multiple overflow venues on the semicircle, at the seminary, and in area churches, that Saturday the university also had baseball, softball, and basketball games scheduled. Streets in town and into town could take no more vehicles. A solid clog of cars choked the two miles to the Y intersection and even beyond another half mile to the turnoff on Route 29 to Nicholasville. Attempting to stem the flow, Jessamine County Emergency Management placed a "Revival at Capacity" flashing road sign at the Y.[25]

"It Was as If the Lord Himself Was the Conductor and There Was No Sheet Music"

That Saturday Mayor Rainwater called President Brown while he was in a cabinet meeting. With the speakerphone on, all concerned discussed what they could possibly do next. All on the call agreed that the city and the Asbury institutions were going to have to do something different. The previous announcement on February 16 that services would be ending on February 23 may have even exacerbated the traffic issue over the second weekend; some may have been especially motivated to come to Wilmore those days for fear of missing the revival. Several larger capacity locations were considered, among them the former Ichthus Festival property and Southland Christian Church in Lexington, but for different reasons these possibilities did not materialize. Meanwhile, Wilmore's Centennial Park came into service for overflow parking, with Free Methodist Church vans called into service to shuttle visitors to campus. Sunday, February 19, witnessed over-capacity crowds as anticipated, but more manageable than Saturday. Mayor Rainwater, on crutches due to an ankle injury, personally directed some three hundred cars onto a city-owned field on the approach to Centennial Park behind his home. From there visitors mostly walked the mile to campus since the available fifteen-passenger vans could not accommodate so many.[26]

With the downward traffic trend on Sunday and Monday, February 19 and 20, the city and Asbury could breathe more freely. Dr. Hay reflected on the challenges of the outpouring:

- For sixteen days the university phone exchange was overwhelmed with calls from all over the country and all over the world. "Eight lines rang all at once 24/7. It was like a radio station was giving away a million dollars."
- Asbury only had one real medical emergency due to a fall. Three or four people fainted in the line, but they did not require an ambulance. "It could have been worse."
- In terms of demands, "When you're piecing it together day to day, it is hard to catch up. It was great, but it was frustrating [because] the goalpost kept moving."
- "Thankfully, God gave us grace," and we had "the dedication and loyalty of all to support each other."
- "We were all so tired, but God still blessed us to get it done."[27]

Glenn Hamilton, to whom Dr. Hay reports, shared in his interview: "For what could have happened, it just didn't." Reminiscing, he said throughout the sixteen days he had fulfilled "a utility player kind of role. I did a lot of logistics and then passed them on to others. It was so fluid and a unique bonding experience [with Asbury staff and volunteers]. It was as if the Lord Himself was the conductor and there was no sheet music."[28]

Dr. Lawson Stone felt blessed by all the superhuman efforts at protection. "Feeling . . . grateful for the people I term the 'sheepdogs': wise and discerning people put in place by the institutions to be vigilant, keeping this season of renewal as a safe place. . . . All you sheepdogs out there, you are doing God's work."[29]

eight

VOLUNTEERS
Labors of Love

All Manner of Gifts

As social media spread word of Asbury's spiritual awakening and as ever-larger numbers of pilgrims began to descend upon Wilmore, the administration came to realize that the university needed help and a lot of it. As an example, President Brown observed a volunteer on scene at 8:00 a.m., and the same person at 1:00 a.m., and again at 8:00 a.m. the next morning—clearly not sustainable.[1] The decision was made to seek and accept all manner of assistance from trusted outside parties. Asbury Seminary, a strategic partner throughout, provided five overflow worship venues: Estes Chapel, McKenna Chapel, the Cowen Building (the former Free Methodist Church sanctuary), and the Sherman Thompson Student Center cafeteria and gymnasium. Several Wilmore pastors also opened their sanctuaries for revival worshippers: Wilmore United Methodist Church/Great Commission Fellowship (the two congregations share worship space), and Mt. Freedom Baptist Church. Other churches provided volunteers including Wilmore Free Methodist Church and a Lexington megachurch, Southland Christian. Its sister megachurch, Southeastern Christian in Louisville, showed up unannounced with a van full of bottled water, just as Asbury was running low.[2]

Lofthouse Collective, a Phoenix-based Christian events management company, donated its services to help coordinate job assignments for the estimated fifteen hundred to eighteen hundred volunteers. In one evening service this writer, while ushering, observed a Lofthouse staffer making multiple trips back and forth between the classroom "Command Center" in Reasoner Hall and the Hughes Lobby in order to coordinate staff and volunteers. Glenn Hamilton was much impressed with Lofthouse: "They were such a gift to us. They came out of nowhere." Four or five of their staff rotated in and out, including the owner, Alisha Files, February 18–23.[3]

Lexington's Joella's Hot Chicken showed up with donated meals, as did Chick-fil-A. The Lexington Salvation Army (colloquially known as Sallies) loaned outdoor space heaters and set up multiple trucks on the semicircle giving away coffee, hot chocolate, water, and hotdogs, as well as one day four hundred Wilmore Subway sandwiches. (Survivors of the press of humanity in Wilmore those days would agree that the Sallies were perfectly justified in classifying this overrun village an emergency deserving their help.) University Director of Development Brad Atkinson, himself a Salvation Army veteran, took Sally hotdogs to those waiting in line, first with his son David, an Asbury undergrad, and then with Erin Grauff, an Asbury student from Oregon, who passed out condiments to go with "the main course." Brad was surprised how "kind and gracious" people were in the incredibly long lines; when he passed out hotdogs near the Miller Communications Building, a full half mile from Hughes as the line looped around the campus, weary pilgrims hugged him.[4]

Donations also arrived in abundance for staff and volunteers who took breaks in the Reasoner Hall "Command Center." Dr. Baldwin recalled on Facebook:

Food arriving unrequested, day in and day out. . . . A beautiful table with flowers and Scripture laid out for us, piled high with every kind of healthy snack. Homemade baked potato soup, a grandma's hummingbird cake, scotchies, homemade cheese balls, vegetable platters, mountains of Chick-fil-A, protein bars, protein drinks, fruit. So much food arriving for students unrequested, 50 pizzas at a time (again and again)!!!, an anonymous Chick-fil-A massive drop-off. . . . A food truck (showing up today!)—"God told me to cook for God's people for free; here I am!"[5]

Communications Professor Heather Hornbeak also took note of the largesse from generous donors: "Today extra-large, industrial-sized, stainless steel pots were filled with roast beef, potatoes, and Mexican rice with chicken in another, fresh fruit, . . . homemade cakes and desserts. . . . There wasn't any indication who had provided the food, but it was clearly someone or business who wanted to nurture those working the event without any recognition. It was like a tithe."[6] Texas Pastor Mark Swayze remembered there were so many "unseen heroes." Dr. Tennent recalled a conversation with several people in the lobby of Hughes Auditorium as Dr. Steve Seamands was comparing the 1970 Asbury Revival with 2023. Out of the blue someone came in with fifteen donated pizzas. Seamands remarked: "We did not have pizzas in 1970!"[7]

Undergirding Prayers

One of the largest categories of volunteers was those involved in prayer for the outpouring. Bud Simon, former TMS Global missionary to Brazil and Asbury Seminary PhD student, identified three categories of prayer initiatives that supported the

Asbury Revival: (1) the visible counselors at the altar in Hughes Auditorium and overflow venues; (2) the behind-the-scenes workers preparing teams prior to their leading worship; and (3) invisible members of the intercessory prayer team. One could actually name a fourth contingent: the training of those serving as altar counselors, a massive undertaking headed by Bud Simon himself.[8] Jessica Avery with the Awakening Project, a college outreach initiated by Dr. David Thomas and Tennessee-based Seedbed, organized the preparation of prayer counselors while Bud Simon conducted the actual two-hour sessions.[9] In sixteen days an estimated seven hundred individuals completed this tutorial to which even retired faculty humbly submitted. Altar workers included current and retired university and seminary administrators, faculty, and staff; current seminary students; staff of Wilmore-based ministries such as the Francis Asbury Society; and pastors and laity from Wilmore and area churches. All those trained to work at the altar wore lanyards, while others wanting to serve as counselors were asked to pray in their seats just with those with whom they came.[10]

Staff and volunteers preparing worship teams in what came to be known as the Consecration Room proved to be a work in progress all sixteen days of the outpouring. In the first few days their recruitment fell to gospel choir director Benjamin Black and his wife, Madeline Black, the chapel coordinator who assists Chaplain Greg Haseloff. Sarah Baldwin called this early-twenties couple "incredible . . . with such grace and wisdom" for their age.[11] With worship continuing day and night and worship team shifts averaging two hours, it proved to be a daunting responsibility to fill all the worship team slots. Many volunteers came from chapel student worship teams, gospel choir members, and university worship ministry majors. But very many additional teams had to be identified and prayed over in order to cover what ended up being 372 hours of continuous, live worship music.[12] Madeline Black wrote in an email: "I don't say this with 100 percent confidence, but it is my sincerest belief that we had worship 24/7 the entire 16 days, and one twelve-hour day (the 23rd). . . . I believe that's 372 hours of continuous worship!"[13] Even when the university began closing Hughes to the public at 1:00 and 2:00 a.m. for cleaning, "night watch" worship teams continued to praise the Lord in song in two-hour shifts through the night.[14] No wonder estimates for the number of individual worship teams range from two hundred to three hundred.[15]

Benjamin and Madeline Black literally depended upon prayers of discernment to guide them to visiting worshippers who were willing and who had musical gifts. Once chosen, new and existing worship team members reported to the Consecration Room, Reasoner Hall 323. There everyone destined for the platform in Hughes—whether musician, singer, or speaker—was the subject of intense prayer for God's anointing and commissioning, typically for an hour before a two-hour time slot.

Relief for the couple came in the form of a missionary who happened to be home in Kentucky on furlough when she first learned of the Asbury Outpouring. Having knowledge of the 1970 Asbury Revival but not knowing a single soul in Wilmore, she drove to Asbury and made her way to the balcony of Hughes Auditorium, where she found herself in tears. At one point, during a previously scheduled prayer time on her phone with her church overseas, she drifted into an empty classroom adjacent to the balcony so as not to disturb worshippers. It happened to be Reasoner Hall 323. When Madeline Black came in to pray with several students preparing to lead worship, this missionary to a restricted access country—Mary, I will call her—offered to leave, but she was told she was welcome to stay and pray with them, which she did with heart and soul. Madeline later recalled: "I didn't know her, but the Holy Spirit was in her." Taxed to the max with all that was on their plates, Madeline and Benjamin shortly delegated leadership of the Consecration Room to Mary, a move many came to see as a God-ordained miracle.[16]

Mary, who is now beloved by many Asburians, did yeomen service, further transforming Reasoner 323 into a sanctuary as well as a room of consecration. "The clock stopped at the door," she remembered. Many prayers enveloped the space, tears sometimes flowed, and worship teams in preparation were made to understand that in Room 323 Jesus was figuratively washing their feet. As Mary explained it, worship teams were to own radical humility in Reasoner 323 so that they could then exalt Jesus from the platform in Hughes. By all accounts the experience for those offering prayers and for those being prayed for was profound. Mary was certain of this: "I will never be the same."[17]

As spiritually transformative as the Consecration Room became, it still was extraordinarily demanding, and there were those who understood Madeline, Ben, and Mary needed more help. That is where Seedbed, the Tennessee-based ministry whose purpose is to help awaken God's people, stepped in. It already was providing dedicated staff, including Sower-in-Chief J. D. Walt and Dr. David Thomas, who assisted Asbury with the critical responsibility of oversight of worship in Hughes.[18] It was also Seedbed, in conjunction with the university, that recruited Mark Swayze, an associate pastor of The Woodlands Methodist Church near Houston, Texas, to help Madeline, Ben, and Mary shepherd worship teams. Pastor Swayze's February 16 Facebook post provides a striking record of the invisible but vital support role of the committed cadre of "worship stewards."

> For 9 straight days at 2 hour increments, college students have led worship at Hughes Auditorium in Wilmore, KY. That's been about 100 worship teams this far. And they don't seem to be ending anytime soon. So [Woodlands worship leader] Brenna [Bullock] and I went to serve. The team organizing all of this needed help [due to

exhaustion]. . . . Their iPhone text group is named the "Worship Stewards." They are a force.

Our first morning [in Wilmore] we . . . experienced what seemed to be a military operation. Everyone is physically exhausted but spiritually on absolute fire. They ask Jesus for wisdom in every decision. No decision for worship is human strategy or planning. They pray, ask Jesus, and then discern together. They speak in turn by raising hands and submitting to one another as they make decisions. It is like nothing I have ever seen before.

They have a process for collecting worship teams. Ready for it? The Holy Spirit highlights people in the room. The "Worship Stewards" then ask those students to lead in a worship band. You will love this next part: This newly formed worship band gets prayed for in the outside hall and then goes to the Consecration Room. Yep. Consecration Room. This is where Spirit-filled hidden "prayer warriors" pray over this newly formed team. This goes on for 30 minutes or more. (This Consecration Room is for any person who will step on the platform, speakers included.) Then the worship team comes back down the stairs, acclimates to the room, and finally after an hour of preparation behind the scenes, switches out with the team on stage that's been leading. The "Worship Stewards" do not want any team to lead worship that has not been prepared in this way.[19]

Pastor Swayze, even with twenty-five years of experience leading worship, shared that once in Wilmore he entered into a unique situation: "I had to relearn doing anything [and] a new way of managing stewardship of what God was doing—in one hour." For starters, he rarely led worship himself—just twice: "This was for young people; there was a favor on Gen Z." Pastor Swayze also totally adopted the worship culture that Madeline, Ben, and Mary were honoring, one centered on "radical humility and radical racial unity." He recalled that those "wanting on stage" very rarely were given that opportunity, including some "world-renowned worship leaders" who volunteered their services.[20] He also appreciated the efforts of Madeline, Ben, and Mary to form worship teams of more than one color. Mary shared that she believed that Pastor Swayze was so flexible, at least in part, because of his experience with COVID-19 which for many months had wrecked corporate worship, his forte. Mary thinks the pandemic was a "detox" that caused Mark to rethink "stage, performance, and celebrity."[21]

So all involved in the Consecration Room were set on the spiritual preparation of musicians—much more concerned for their spiritual dedication than their musical performance. Most were ad hoc teams that had never played together before and were lucky to have had any time to look over the playlist of 129 choruses and hymns (see appendix C). As a result, many teams were less than recording material, but before worshippers they modeled purest praise to the Lord. By that criterion, by all accounts, they helped lead thousands to the throne of God's grace.[22]

In addition to the visible altar prayers of counselors and penitents and the behind-the-scenes prayers of the Consecration Room, another invisible source of petitions heading heavenward came from an intercessory prayer room on the ground floor of Hughes Auditorium. For months, missionary to Colombia Jeannine Brabon had prayed for renewal prior to the 1970 Asbury Revival and was a student leader in that outpouring; then in 2023, once again, she was alternately a counselor at the altar and among those intercessors in a classroom underneath the chapel petitioning for God's mercies for those upstairs. When a Chilean family testified to having sold their car to pay for airfare to Asbury, Jeannine was the volunteer on the platform translating for them. Otherwise, she was mostly in the background downstairs calling upon the Lord to continue his work of revival. Other prayer intercessors included an Asbury Seminary biblical scholar, volunteers from the Billy Graham Evangelistic Association, and five prayer teams from Houston-area Woodlands Methodist Church. In addition, Francis Asbury Society's Titus Women offered prayers for the outpouring remotely.[23]

Vice President Glenn Hamilton shared that a Hispanic pilgrim from Boston gave him a small metal canister filled with handwritten prayer requests in Spanish. She asked if he would have someone at Asbury lift these petitions to the Lord. He promised it would happen, and he delivered these prayer requests to the Intercessory Prayer Room. Touched by the spiritual hunger that this entreaty represented, Hamilton wondered what happened to the Boston prayer canister. It found its way to Dr. Sarah Baldwin's office, where he was able to retrieve it. They will be translated into English, he shared—one copy for the archives and one copy for himself as a tangible reminder of earnest seekers from Boston.[24]

"Job Descriptions" Unending

At the outset of Asbury's February 2023 spiritual renewal, volunteers came forward to help without being asked, saw a need, and set to it. But as word spread and lines lengthened to enter Hughes, coordination of helping hands was a must. President Brown told a *Christianity Today* reporter:

> There were 100 people volunteering at any one time [as it turned out, a lowball estimate] just to make these services work on the fly. There was a classroom that got redeployed into almost a command center. If you walked in, there were flow charts on the wall and the whiteboards were covered with information. There was a volunteer check-in station. . . . It was one of the most impressive technical feats I've ever seen.[25]

Early on, without being asked, an Asbury student set up a tea and coffee table. As Baldwin relates: "She took it on herself (she said Jesus called her to it), to make coffee for hundreds with two Keurigs. She ran out of cups and prayed for more cups. She got more cups."[26] A Lexington Alliance Church member baked enough banana bread to rejuvenate some thirty teens who had been standing in the Hughes line for hours.[27] As a labor of love, another woman from Indianapolis baked chocolate chip cookies for a full day, drove to Wilmore, and delivered them to Asbury herself. Dr. Jonathan Raymond met this lady one night in front of his home on Kinlaw Drive as she was pulling a cart loaded with her cookies. Dr. Raymond did not know how far beyond his home she had parked, but her trek to Asbury's campus was at least half a mile.[28]

Others made purchases at Costco and drove a loaded van to Wilmore to feed staff and pilgrims. The women's auxiliary of Nicholasville's Edgewood Baptist Church sent food. A church in Mt. Sterling, Kentucky, called Little Caesar's in nearby Nicholasville, purchased seventy pizzas, and had them delivered to the campus. This happened several times according to Glenn Hamilton. Tearing up, he recalled running low on water for those waiting in line when pallets of bottled water appeared, unanticipated but greatly appreciated.[29] Provost Sherry Powers tells of someone coming up to her in Morrison Hall, informing her that the women's restroom was out of toilet paper. Just then a truck pulled up and unloaded pallets of water, paper towels, and—that's right—toilet paper. It was more of Glenn Hamilton's "just in time." The provost was sure "The Lord knew what we needed."[30]

Though no part of his job description, President Kevin Brown was seen pulling a wagon with food for pilgrims standing in the line to enter Hughes. He was surprised by "the incredible sweet spirit of men and women waiting in the cold. It was unlike what I would expect." Despite the long wait, the line was happy, so the president was happy. Another surprise was a food vendor who showed up with his truck and began giving away hot dogs. He was only planning to stay for a day, but he received so many unsolicited donations that he came back three or four more days with his free-for-all hotdogs.[31] Others donated barbeque, soup, and cakes.[32] Hospitality "miracle workers," some known and many unknown, purchased every bottle of water in Lexington's two Sam's Clubs for the benefit of spiritual pilgrims to Wilmore.[33] Glenn Hamilton, Hughes worship speaker David Thomas, and Asbury retiree volunteer Jeannette Davis all independently shared that the "miracle of provisions" reminded them of Jesus's feeding the five thousand with a handful of loaves and fishes.[34]

Volunteer roles were diverse to say the least. An unknown number of Wilmore residents took in houseguests on short notice, including Sam and Rachel Powdrill who hosted twenty-five overnight, none of whom spoke English. Retired missionary to Korea, Bette Crouse, housed thirty-two sojourners over a span of two weeks, including an NBC reporter.[35] Vice President Mark Whitworth got home late one night to learn nine pilgrims were spending the night, only two of whom he knew.[36]

Tech veterans of Ichthus (the former Wilmore-based Christian music festival) came forward with helping hands to assist Asbury University IT staff who were completely maxed out.[37] Dr. Tennent shared that one day a Wilmore resident showed up in Asbury Seminary's Morrison Administration Building, someone who had never had any ties to the seminary or the university. She came with her vacuum cleaner in tow and asked how she could help. Her labor of love was sweeping the carpets in Estes Chapel, which Dr. Tennent said needed her touch.[38] One Asbury Seminary student, a Methodist youth pastor from Zimbabwe, found he could serve by directing those new to Wilmore to restrooms and thirty-six portable toilets placed beside Kinlaw Library by the Asbury semicircle.[39] Someone else set up a baby changing station outside a Hughes restroom; "Not your typical equipment here!" remarked Professor Nicholson. "This is the body of Christ working across institutional lines to support a movement of God. How beautiful is the Kingdom of God!"[40]

From Wilmore Free Methodist Church alone came remote parking van drivers, at least half a dozen altar counselors, and Keith Madill, a retired school administrator cleaning bathrooms in Hughes. When asked what the highlight of the revival was for him, the response was: "I am just thrilled to be here to help."[41] Free Methodist Senior Pastor Daryl Diddle and his wife, Annette, could be found doing bag checks near the steps of Hughes, and Associate Pastor Dwight Winter volunteered as a shuttle bus driver.[42]

One Wilmore Free Methodist regular attendee is Dr. Jonathan Raymond, retired president of British Columbia's Trinity Western University. At the start of the spiritual awakening, he focused on intercessory prayer in his home, but "I could not stay away." He spent some time in Hughes, but more often he walked the long line of visitors offering encouragement to those waiting to enter Hughes Auditorium. On one occasion he talked with a mother and son who had arrived from Indiana at 11:00 a.m. and were just about to enter Hughes at 8:00 p.m. On another occasion in the Asbury Seminary gymnasium overflow venue, he prayed with a Hispanic family dealing with serious father-son frictions, a family that experienced a degree of healing and restitution through this retired president's prayer.[43]

Sarah Baldwin posted: "Most of the people coming have no idea that their usher navigating a wheelchair through the rain has a PhD, and their prayer minister is a retired seminary professor. It was radical humility and radical hospitality."[44]

Asbury students at the altar in Hughes Auditorium. Student Life Vice President Sarah Baldwin praying over anxious Gen Z youth. February 9 or 10, 2023. Courtesy of Asbury University.

Visitors in line to enter Hughes Memorial Auditorium. Also present are Salvation Army relief vehicles dispensing food, hot drinks, and water. February 17, 2023. Courtesy of Asbury University.

Worshippers kneeling on the semicircle lawn with Kinlaw Library, Hughes Auditorium, and Morrison Hall in the background (left to right). February 17, 2023. Courtesy of Asbury University.

A view of the long line to enter Hughes Auditorium and the large number of visitors on the semicircle lawn. University and seminary buildings in the background. February 17, 2023. Courtesy of Lisa Weaver-Swartz.

Aerial view of the Asbury University campus with a portion of the Asbury Seminary campus in the foreground. Includes the line to enter Hughes Auditorium from the semicircle and to enter Estes Chapel along North Lexington Avenue. February 18, 2023. Courtesy of Asbury University.

Worshippers in 1,500 seat Hughes Auditorium. A view from the platform. February 19, 2023. Courtesy of Asbury University.

Guys with arms on each others' shoulders in worship in Hughes Auditorium, February 19, 2023. Courtesy of Asbury University.

Crowds on the semicircle lawn facing a simulcast screen of worship in Hughes Auditorium. Asbury Seminary Library is in the background. February 18, 2023. Courtesy of Asbury University.

Counseling and hands-on prayer for one seeking more of God on the semicircle lawn. February 19, 2023. Courtesy of Asbury University.

Worshippers from near and far on the semicircle lawn. Asbury Seminary's Morrison Administration Building in background. February 19, 2023. Courtesy of Asbury University.

nine

MEDIA COVERAGE
From *The Collegian* to TikTok

News of Asbury's 1970 revival was spread by word of mouth, students phoning home, hundreds of student witness teams fanning out to colleges and churches across the nation, and broadcasts of three Lexington TV stations.[1] But in 2023 the university found itself coping with a flood of media outlets,[2] including CBN, CNN, NBC, and three nights of Fox News coverage, including Tucker Carlson's three nights of favorable, if a bit bewildered, commentary. To keep the outpouring a strictly spiritual renewal, the university politely declined Carlson's proposal to travel to Wilmore. Despite being turned down, his on-air response on February 17 was quite charitable:

> When you meet people who don't want publicity, they are either doing something wrong or, in the rarest of occasions, they're doing something right . . . so right and so beautiful and true that media coverage cannot enhance it. It would only detract from it. We think that's what is happening at Asbury University. God bless them for turning us down.[3]

Mark Whitworth, appointed to his post just three years prior, was in place "just in time" to handle the media blitz. He previously had worked for decades for the Southeastern Conference sports juggernaut, most recently as its associate commissioner, experience that served Asbury well in managing crowds as well as media, 2023.[4]

Traditional print reporting ranged from the *Asbury Collegian* student paper—out first on February 8 and exceptionally competent for an undergrad enterprise—to leading national dailies including the *Washington Post* and the *New York Times*, to news magazines including *Time, The Atlantic,* and *The Economist,* to large circulation evangelical periodicals including *Christianity Today* and *Decision Magazine*.[5] Word of the revival traveled as well by phone, text, and email. Unauthorized smartphone videos, which spread like wildfire, also did much to publicize the revival. For the first ten days of the outpouring, Asbury's communications staff livestreamed only regularly scheduled chapel services, then on February 19 extended its own livestreaming of limited portions of worship in Hughes beginning that evening.[6]

Electronic platforms through which news of the Asbury spiritual awakening spread included blogs, Facebook, YouTube, websites, Twitter, and TikTok. In 2013 Asbury Seminary's First Fruits Press website, that affords free downloads for all its titles, published an expanded second edition of Robert Coleman's *One Divine Moment* on the 1970 Asbury Revival, coedited with Dr. David Gyertson. While in January 2023 this title registered 9 downloads, 488 copies were downloaded in February 2023 in the wake of Asbury's most recent spiritual renewal that month.[7]

Total likes for Asbury's Facebook page increased from approximately 10,600 on February 8 to 43,456 as of April 6, for a better-than-threefold percentage increase during and since the revival. Even more telling, Asbury's Facebook page reach for February 8–23 was 15,600,444, with the top five page-audience cities being Lexington, Nicholasville, Wilmore, and Louisville, Kentucky, and surprisingly, Addis Ababa, Ethiopia. Instagram reach for February 8–23 was 518,727. Two of the top five Instagram cities were Lexington and Wilmore, Kentucky, with again a surprise, the other top three cities being São Paulo, Rio de Janeiro, and Curitiba, Brazil. The views for the top five "Asbury Revival" YouTube videos as of April 6 were 1.7 million; 1.6 million; 1.3 million; 883,000; and 881,000—for a total of 6,340,000 (in round numbers), not counting other "Asbury Revival" hashtags.[8] As for Twitter, one tweet that stood out among the thousands was that of former vice president Mike Pence who shared he was "deeply moved to see the revival taking place @AsburyUniv!"[9]

Still, no social media platform came close to matching the viral reach of the Asbury spiritual awakening provided by TikTok. Already on February 9 the hashtag #asburyrevival garnered 10 million views; 24.4 million by February 15; 35.8 million by February 16; 63 million by February 18; 68.1 million by February 19; and a conservative figure of 240.8 million by April 6. The figure is conservative because not all variants of Asbury Revival hashtags are included, nor the more generic Asbury hashtag with views of 76.9 million as of April 6, an unknown portion of which relate to the revival.[10] What makes the Asbury Revival social media reach all the more striking is the fact that the university did not promote it. Rather, as noted, it actively (but unsuccessfully) discouraged iPhone recordings and livestreaming of Hughes services for fear they would distract from worship or might not protect students giving sensitive public confessions.

A helpful demonstration of the impact of social media upon Asbury's spiritual renewal comes from the journal of university communications professor Heather Hornbeak, who taught a course on interactive media during the outpouring. She revised her syllabus to include a module on social media dynamics, using Asbury's spiritual renewal in progress as a case study. Quite active on the cyber front, she monitored the reach of the Asbury Revival on social media; facilitated logistics for those desiring to travel to Wilmore; and advised the administration when she discovered that some of President Brown's internal communications were somehow finding their way onto social media platforms. This very busy Professor Hornbeak also joined various unofficial online "Asbury Revival" groups to correct misinformation and to provide updates on accommodations, worship schedules, overflow venues, etc. These groups, with no connection to the university or the seminary, were multiplying by the day. They ranged in size from hundreds to thousands of members. It took Professor Hornbeak two days to join one group because it was receiving close to five thousand requests to join per day. By February 20 five groups alone with "Asbury" and "Revival" in their titles had a combined membership of more than seventy-five thousand, with more joining daily.[11]

During the revival, instead of continuing with volunteering in person between classes, Professor Hornbeak shifted to two hours per day helping where needed, and the remainder of the day working with students, then laptop research at night:

> I spent much of my time scanning social media, answering questions with logistical information, sending resources, copying and pasting parts of Dr. Brown's [public] statements as answers to questions, links to unlisted accommodations, campus maps, and more. I was a librarian on social media for 10 days.[12]

Class discussions on social media scenarios included:

> using the instance of the in-real-time event happening just a few feet away. You could see through our window the swarms of people gathering just outside our quiet classroom. . . . I reminded them that the uniqueness of our social media goals were much like Howard Dayton's

approach in business. Our business school is named after him. Most program objectives involve the effort to improve profits, but Howard Dayton and Asbury believe there is something deeper and more complex to offer the marketplace in addition.[13]

Meanwhile, people on social media were clamoring for livestreaming of Hughes worship by the university rather than pirated phone video of varying quality. Professor Hornbeak noted that "the environment online was getting ugly." Asbury's attempt to protect student testimonies and worship from outside distraction was falling short. Clandestine phone recordings, despite signs all over Hughes prohibiting them, "were getting thousands of followers with millions of views. . . . With the largest crowd to date [February 19], it became apparent Asbury had no other option but to livestream in order to control the pouring in of people."[14]

The next day in class Professor Hornbeak recounted "a media story less than twenty-four hours old." Using Google Analytics she showed students that Asbury's first night of livestreaming went viral. At 10:00 p.m. the night before, with Asbury communications staff inaugurating livestreaming, "there was a spike in page views," an increase of more than 1,000 percent in only a few minutes. She had the evidence that many viewers were engaging "for a lengthy three hours" at a time. "The ones watching hung on to every minute."[15]

Professor Hornbeak had developed trust with many online groups with no connections in Wilmore by providing accurate information on the outpouring. Her efforts now paid off: "I watched the Google Analytics traffic map bubbles all over the world become larger . . . in places I had built trust. . . . The notifications of likes, comments, and shares were a non-stop pinging noise as I worshipped, watching the livestream online." Within three hours this volunteer "social media librarian" and

Asbury Revival expediter had "500 shares on one announcement alone. This single post's reach (total number of shares) announcing the official livestream is a number so large it is difficult to accurately calculate."

The dramatic increase in international travelers to Asbury the last week of the outpouring undoubtedly was a function of social media in general and Asbury's decision to livestream.[16]

ten

WILMORE

Blessed but Overwhelmed

On Sunday, February 19, cars were so backed up from Wilmore past the *Y* intersection and onto US 68 that state police had to divert traffic, steering it to a less-congested alternate route to Asbury's campus.[1] Cars, vans, even buses full of college students, poured into two-traffic-light Wilmore, population six thousand. "There were cars parked everywhere, even in many places where they shouldn't," recalled Asbury Seminary Professor Ben Witherington.[2] His seminary colleague, Lawson Stone, recalled: "It's hilarious to be driving around Wilmore looking for a parking place. . . . Folks coming in to experience the season of renewal at Asbury have taken almost every parking place in town. How often do you 'rejoice' that you can't find a parking space? It's just wonderful."[3] But when visitors began parking in people's yards without permission, some residents began to feel "invaded" and "unsafe."[4]

"It was crazy and exciting at the same time," Steve Rehner wrote in an email to friends. On some days, out-of-state cars parked in front of his house, nearly a mile from Asbury's Hughes Auditorium, with hundreds of cars even farther afield.[5] The city's Centennial Park and the Wilmore Free Methodist Church

(1.5 miles and .9 miles respectively from campus) became temporary overflow parking locations, with volunteers providing shuttle van service to the revival. Mayor Harold Rainwater, who has been in office longer than any mayor in the state of Kentucky (forty-six years), declared he had never seen anything like the congestion of February 2023 in Wilmore.[6] Plenty of residents objected to the crowds, while others stepped forward as volunteers. Rehner, who shuttled visitors from Centennial Park to campus for some four hours one afternoon, shared: "It was a blessing to hear from so many of them, where they were from, and how the Lord had led them to come and be refreshed in His Presence."[7]

Estimates for the total number of spiritual sojourners who descended upon Wilmore, February 9–23, range from 20,000 to 100,000, with Chaplain Greg Haseloff's estimate of 70,000 appearing to be most likely. To this total add 6,000 Wilmore residents and 1,112 and 555 university and seminary residential and commuter students, respectively, for an estimated total of 77,667 living or sojourning in the village during February 8–23, 2023. So many visitors sought to be part of Asbury's spiritual awakening that the university had to scramble to arrange multiple overflow venues. In addition to Hughes (capacity 1,500), Asbury Seminary made available Estes Chapel (seating 660), McKenna Chapel (seating 375), and the Sherman Thompson Student Center gymnasium (seating approximately 1,000) and cafeteria, each supplied with altars, seminary prayer teams, and simulcasts of Hughes worship. The second weekend Estes, McKenna, and the seminary gym were at capacity both February 18 and 19.[8]

When Estes Chapel was at capacity, Dr. Tennent had his "Moses" lead hundreds of spiritual pilgrims to McKenna Chapel.[9] Two churches that are walking distance from Hughes also opened their doors for simulcast livestreaming from Hughes: Wilmore United Methodist Church/Great Commission Fellowship (February 14–19) and Mount Freedom Baptist Church

(February 17–19). The much smaller Wilmore Christian Church also opened for prayer. A symbolic visual illustration of the unity of spirit of the Asbury institutions came during a regularly scheduled worship hour in the seminary's Estes Chapel on February 9. At one point during the service everyone turned around in their pews to face toward the university and prayed for God's continued blessing on the outpouring.[10]

Asbury Seminary President Timothy Tennent observed an inner and outer core to the awakening. There was an inner core of Gen Z youth seeking more of God, especially in the early days and especially in Hughes; then there was an outer, much larger core of seekers after God's mercy and healing, seemingly from everywhere.[11] It was this outer core that Dr. Tennent considered the seminary's primary field of ministry—even though many seminary faculty and students also volunteered to help the university host the outpouring.

Early on Dr. Tennent told his cabinet and staff how to respond to requests for help from the university: "Find a way to say yes." Perhaps he was motivated in part by his own "awakening in the 1970s which totally changed the direction of [his] life." In conversation with President Kevin Brown, Dr. Tennent asked, "Do you need money?" That was not the great need; rather, it was space. (The seminary came through with so many additional worship venues that in the final days of the outpouring a larger number of visitors over age twenty-five found places to worship across Lexington Avenue from the university.)[12] Perhaps the most dramatic instance of the seminary's "radical hospitality" came on Saturday, February 18, the second weekend of the outpouring when thousands of sojourners were pouring into an over-capacity Wilmore. Dr. Brown and Dr. David Thomas asked Dr. Tennent if the seminary gym might serve as another venue for worship. The answer was yes, and in two and a half hours seminary staff postponed intramural sports, spread a tarp over the basketball court, set up one thousand chairs and an altar, with two simulcast screens on loan from Lexington's Southland Christian Church on very short notice.[13]

Paul Dupree, IT director for the university, could not give the seminary community enough compliments for its generous help "over and over again." According to Dupree, seminary staff reached out to him and did almost all the simulcast logistics for the various seminary overflow venues. Only for the seminary gym did the university play a role in the setup. With so many pressing IT requirements day after day, the seminary's help "freed us up," Dupree recalled with gratitude. "It was really miraculous. When I talk about it, I get emotional." Another gift Dupree recalled came in the midst of one of many ad hoc IT staff task discussions in the Reasoner Hall "Command Center." An older African American lady he had never met came up to him and asked if she could pray for him there and then. Under great pressure, as most all staff were those sixteen days in February, Dupree said yes. (His prayer intercessor is president of a ministry based in Pearland, Texas.) Not one to show great emotion in public, Asbury's exhausted head of IT found himself weeping as he was being ministered to by a bold personality doing her part to hold Asbury's revival gently and prayerfully.[14]

Lines for visitors to enter Hughes Auditorium grew to unheard-of lengths, at its peak half a mile long. At first the line meandered across the campus semicircle lawn. Then as crowds continued to increase it was redirected, stretching along the semicircle sidewalk past Morrison Hall, Hager Administration Building, Glide-Crawford Dormitory, then around the dorm onto College Avenue, past the back of Johnson Cafeteria, as far as the Miller Communications Building, nearly lapping the central campus. Depending upon the day and hour, reports of waiting times in this line ranged from four to ten hours, and many pilgrims never made it into Hughes.[15]

Sometimes it was sunny, sometimes rainy (February 16 and 23), one day, snowing. The night of February 16 Free Methodist Pastor Daryl Diddle and his wife, Annette, recalled: "We walked back the length of the line to let people know that the wait would be quite long and to invite/encourage them to consider going to the other sanctuaries/chapels to view the simulcast. Hardly any went. They were happy to wait for Hughes."[16] On one occasion volunteers Keith and Jenny Madill spoke with the last four hundred people in line yard by yard, sharing with them that, unfortunately, they were unlikely to be able to enter Hughes that night.[17] Asbury IT staff set up two large screens facing the semicircle for livestreaming of worship inside Hughes. At times those gathered in the semicircle numbered in the thousands, in addition to those in line and visitors across Lexington Avenue on Asbury Seminary grounds.[18]

For the town of Wilmore, as noted, the revival was a mixed blessing. On the positive side is the report of Randy Rainwater, an Asbury College grad and senior pastor of Grace New Hope Church, Lawrenceville, Georgia, who returned on news of the revival: "There were no fights, no violence, and no arrests. State, county, and city police worked to serve and keep safety. No consumerism was allowed—no permits were given to food trucks, existing businesses sold food, and everything else was given away."

Pastor Rainwater continued:

Of everyone in Wilmore, the person most impacted by the crowds would have been Leonard Fitch. He owns and works the local [IGA] grocery store. His parking lot was so full no one seeking groceries could park. My brother Harold Rainwater, who is the forty-six-year mayor of Wilmore, called him to check on him. Harold and his wife Sherry have worked nonstop to keep things safe, caring for the city and the "sojourner" seeking a temporary home in Wilmore. Leonard acknowledged the struggle, and Harold asked if the city could help. Leonard said, "Harold, don't change anything; my store is not as important as this revival; this is what I have been praying for." . . . Leonard was my first boss, and I am grateful for that. The revival . . . was already in Leonard. Not everything I learned from the revival I learned in Hughes; some of it I learned from Leonard.[19]

How many grocery stores in the US choose not to sell alcohol or tobacco and are closed on Sundays? And I doubt there is any grocer/lay pastor in the US who conducts more funerals for the churched and the unchurched than Leonard Fitch. He is IGA's and Asbury University's (class of '64) salt of the earth.

What led Wilmore and the Asbury institutions to deal with massive inconvenience so charitably? Pastor Randy Rainwater, former town kid, has the answer:

> Leviticus 19:33–34 [ESV] tells us the way we treat the refugee, or the sojourner seen by God; it's a little ominous, actually: "When a stranger sojourns with you in your land, you shall not do him wrong. You shall treat the stranger who sojourns with you as the native among you, and you shall love him as yourself, for you were strangers in the land of Egypt: I am the LORD your God."[20]

So Wilmore's and Asbury's hospitality serves as a marker of spiritual renewal just as does the penitents at the altar in Hughes Auditorium.

eleven

SPREADING NEAR AND FAR
"Come, Tarry, Go"

Asbury University President Kevin Brown recognized that only time would tell the full impact of the gift of spiritual renewal that was bestowed upon the Asbury institutions, Wilmore, and the wider world in the wake of February 2023. But he is certain of this fact, that a deep hunger exists near and far for a new and fresh "divine moment" with the Almighty. In his February 16 communiqué he invoked Jesus's Beatitude: "Blessed are those who hunger and thirst for righteousness, for they will be filled" (Matt. 5:6).[1] Others sense the same. Professor Suzanne Nicholson wrote: "The thousands of visitors to campus have only demonstrated how much spiritual thirst exists right now. These people are desperate for relief, life, and hope, and they are willing to wait in line for hours to enter the place where the veil between heaven and earth is remarkably thin right now."[2] Similarly, Eric Allen, Kentucky Baptist Convention missions team leader, saw it as self-evident that "People are hungry to see God at work, and I think that's what draws the crowds."[3]

Working with others leading worship in Hughes was a life-changing experience for Vice President Sarah Baldwin, chiefly because she witnessed a world of hunger and hurt coming to the altar:

> As theologians and, well, everyone everywhere name and debate what it was and wasn't, what I do know for sure is that people are longing for God. . . . [They are] so hungry that they wait for hours in freezing temperatures because they want to be at the altar. As I look out over the crowd in Hughes, I see and hear broken-down people, small children, people in wheelchairs, young people with stories of addiction, moms who are crying over their children in rehab, and shining faces who want so badly to see Jesus and who seem to be deeply experiencing an outpouring of the love of God.[4]

For Dr. David Thomas, co-laborer with Dr. Baldwin on the Hughes platform, "It was not hunger; it was starvation." And those who sought the Lord were rewarded. Dr. Thomas—and others—noted that many entering Hughes after hours in line did not take seats but made their way directly to the altar.[5]

Provost Sherry Powers arrived on campus very early one morning, possibly Friday of the second weekend, February 17. She was stunned by the masses of people on campus. In our interview in her office, Dr. Powers got up and looked out one of her two windows where she recalled seeing the line that had stretched from Hughes the length of the semicircle, around Glide-Crawford Dormitory, and before her eyes on College Avenue. She then walked behind her desk to her second window and recalled having witnessed that same line far distant turning from College Avenue onto Main Street (Route 1268) toward the Miller Communications Building. She could have told me, but instead she acted out her early-morning dismay. As Dr. Powers relived the view out her windows, she remembered the miracle of Jesus feeding the five thousand: "These people are hungry for the

Lord." Overcome, more Scripture came to mind: "Feed my sheep" [John 21:17].[6]

Asbury graduate and Wesley Biblical Seminary professor Andy Miller III interviewed the Salvation Army's Diane Ury, who counseled many stricken, then joyful, penitents in McKenna Chapel and Hughes Auditorium. One senses the depth and breadth of the Asbury renewal as she burst with excitement sharing with podcast listeners God's healing touch as she ministered at the altar with hungry souls.[7]

Renewal volunteer and Wilmore Free Methodist Senior Pastor Daryl Diddle also came to sense deep spiritual yearning as he and his wife worked security and walked the long line of those patiently waiting to enter Hughes:

> Annette and I talked to hundreds of people from all over the country. They were all extremely kind and appreciative and amazed at what God was doing. One conclusion I reached is that there are many very spiritually dry places in our land—with people who are genuinely seeking a word from the Lord. It reminded me that, despite our communities' weaknesses and needs, we live in a very spiritually rich place and probably don't appreciate enough of God's presence.[8]

Professor Craig Keener recalled:

> When I first saw the lines extended across the front of the campus and up its side, I felt like I was living in an alternate reality. It reminded me, however, of how Jesus had compassion for the crowds. Volunteers guided the crowds and provided water.[9]

On campus every night, Asbury Seminary President Timothy Tennent sensed "a broad spiritual hunger in the country. . . . Trust is low; there is a sense of desperation." Yet people from out of town did not complain about the long lines. They also seemed to hold their denominational affiliations lightly, if they held them at all. Dr. Tennent concluded that most of those waiting in lines were quite oblivious to denominational allegiances. Most, he believed, had no prior knowledge of the Asbury institutions' Wesleyan tradition. In that sense it was "not a Methodist revival."[10]

Almost instantaneous fellowships of pilgrims coalesced among the "waiters." One night, Dr. Tennent met a woman standing in line with a walker. She was obviously in pain but determined to stay the course. Her fellowship of pilgrim partners, strangers just hours before, were excited for her as Dr. Tennent arranged for her to "break the line." They were not upset that she would make it inside straight away without them. She just had one request of the seminary president: Could her father who was with her in line accompany her? "He's not a Christian." The answer was yes.[11]

Asbury University Vice President Mark Troyer had a similar experience. He came across an expectant mother, eight months pregnant, cold, and on her feet for hours. In front of the Hager Administration Building, still a good one hundred yards from Hughes, she was in the midst of her own "congregation" of spiritual pilgrims—a pastor and his wife from Washington, DC; a family from Tennessee; and a mother and daughter from New Mexico. With Dr. Troyer's help and the blessing of her super-patient line companions, this mother-to-be was ushered into Hughes posthaste.[12] In another case a policeman arranged for a couple with two small children to enter Hughes early.[13] Vice President Mark Whitworth, on occasion in the lobby of Hughes, was struck by "the sense of anticipation on the faces" of those entering the auditorium after hours of standing in line.[14]

Accounts abound of exceptional odysseys undertaken to be part of Asbury's spiritual renewal. A husband and wife, professors at a Christian university, drove through the night to be a part of the revival, and to extend their stay, slept the next night in their car.[15] Another couple was so spiritually hungry they loaded their small children in a van and drove across country to stand in line for hours in the cold.[16] College student Bryce Balico drove 660 miles from Philadelphia to Wilmore in ten and a half hours.[17] Sophia Grover, a Virginia Tech University freshman biological systems engineering major, drove six hours with members of her campus Bible study group for a twelve-hour window of worship in Hughes. She was surprised to meet someone from Brazil and another worshipper who had flown into Lexington on a one-way ticket bound for Asbury.[18] J. T. Reeves, a senior at Chicago-area Wheaton College, learned of Asbury's spiritual renewal from an Instagram video and from a campus chapel where "there was an encouragement to pay attention to a move of the Lord in Asbury." That day he made it to Hughes Auditorium in six and a half hours.[19] Having made many road trips between Wheaton and Wilmore, this writer can attest J. T. must have been flying low!

Nick Hall of Pulse ministry was another of the pilgrims who first heard of the Asbury Revival from Instagram and who bought a one-way ticket, this one from Minneapolis to Lexington.[20] Barry Maracle and Toyin Crandell drove fourteen hours from Canada to Wilmore. Bible expositor David Legge from Ireland was in London's Heathrow Airport bound for Little Rock, Arkansas, when he first heard word of extraordinary worship on the campus of Asbury University. Once in the US he changed his plans, drove nine hours from Arkansas to Kentucky, "got a hotel [in Lexington], and stood in line for an hour to get in [Hughes]. And the line is double or triple in size today."[21]

As previously mentioned, a couple from Chile sold their car in order to pay for flights to Asbury, only to be literally showered with money when strangers worshipping in Hughes learned of their saga.[22] One worshipper came up to Dr. Sarah Baldwin and gave her money: "Can you give it to the lady who sold the car?"

Her answer was yes. The second weekend of the outpouring a couple from Russia arrived with their three boys, knowing very little English. Though it was the peak of sojourners in Wilmore, police managed to arrange for their entrance into Hughes where Asbury staffer Jeannie Banter prayed with them at the altar.[23]

Nearly as far afield was a pilgrim from Riga, Latvia, who flew to the US on a ticket already purchased for Seattle, rented a car, and drove cross-country to Wilmore. On the campus semicircle lawn Vice President Mark Troyer came across this Latvian sojourner who was distraught over not having been given an opportunity to speak in Hughes Auditorium. He was also anxious to record an interview with someone from Asbury to share with his church and media back in Riga. Dr. Troyer, who accommodated his new brother in Christ with a three-minute video account of Asbury's spiritual renewal, learned later that two veteran counselors had an extended season of prayer with this visitor from Latvia before his departure.[24]

Pastor Bill Elliff shared another account of folk making their way to worship in Wilmore:

> Thousands are taking quick, modern-day pilgrimages to Wilmore, Kentucky, to see what God is doing. While I was there on the third day following its outbreak, I had booked a hotel room for several days but felt led to leave after three days. I went to check out, and a man was checking in.
>
> "Are you coming for the revival?" I asked.
>
> "Yes," he replied.
>
> "How long are you staying?"
>
> "Two days."
>
> "Well, take my room. I've already paid for those days."
>
> "That's awesome!" said the hotel receptionist.
>
> "By the way," I asked, "Where are you from?"
>
> "I drove ten hours from Toronto, Canada."

"That's amazing," I said. "I drove ten hours from Arkansas."

Like moths to a flame, we were drawn from north and south just like others from around the nation (and now, around the world).

One Lexington hotel receptionist told Pastor Elliff the weekend of February 11–12 every room was taken: "We were not prepared for revival," she said. Elliff thought to himself, "May it not be true of us."[25]

Even with Wilmore's unprecedented congestion and the long lines to enter Hughes, volunteers were surprised how calmly most sojourners took the inconvenience. Reverend Max Vanderpool, who volunteered numerous hours during the February spiritual awakening, is a part-time Asbury instructor and pastor of the Generations Church in nearby Nicholasville. He called to mind the fitting analogy of Catholic pilgrimages, past and present:

> There seems to be value in making a pilgrimage. Why? You journey to a "holy place" to encounter God, but you often find that God meets you on the way. This is the testimony of so many people (who traveled as individuals or couples). They met other pilgrims in line from distant places. They found they had much in common. They prayed together. And they journeyed together into Hughes Auditorium.[26]

At a Nicholasville ministerial meeting, Fr. Justin Patterson of St. Athanasius Orthodox Church remarked to Pastor Vanderpool, "You Protestants have re-invented the pilgrimage." Having met sojourners from Portugal, England, Brazil, and Uganda in Hughes, Vanderpool agreed: "I've watched it unfold every night at Asbury."[27] Many making their way to Wilmore came to recognize it is the spiritual journey as well as the destination.

In keeping with the gospel admonitions, "Come, Tarry, Go," in the stained glass window of the Wilmore United Methodist Church, the point of any spiritual revitalization is not to put a light under a bushel, but, as Jesus taught, to let the light shine (see Matt. 5:15–16). As Asbury University President Kevin Brown put it: "The trajectory of renewal meetings is always outward."[28] Robert Kanary, retired United Methodist minister and author of *Spontaneous Revivals*, has pointed out that initially the Asbury awakening of 2023 "was centrifugal (attracting people to the center), rather than centripetal (inspiring teams as in past Asbury revivals to go out to tell the story)."[29] But due to social media, word of renewal by all accounts spread more quickly and farther than ever before. Modern means of communication drew thousands to Hughes for worship and personal spiritual renewal.

A minister from Pennsylvania well illustrated the pull and push, the "come, tarry, and go" of the Asbury renewal of 2023:

> My 13-year-old son, Ezra, and I jumped in a vehicle and drove 8+ hours to Wilmore, KY, and the campus of Asbury University on Sunday after I finished preaching in both of our services here in Clearfield, PA. We had finalized this plan only the afternoon prior, agreeing to embark on this adventure together to participate in at least a couple of hours of what we'd been reading and seeing reports of via social media. . . .
>
> As I recalled and re-read accounts of the 1970 Asbury Revival, I remembered studying this event while studying at Indiana Wesleyan [University] as a ministerial student in the late-90s. I remember thinking then how I would've liked to have been able to have participated in what took place in the 70s. That thought triggered the "Why not now?" question and an internal back-and-forth of if/how/why follow-up questions.

Saying YES to going was a significant step for me. Last week, as I began to hear the murmur of this "continued chapel service at Asbury," I committed to praying specifically that the Lord would continue to pour himself out THERE (at Asbury) and HERE (in me!). I felt the tug of wanting to be "in the room where it happens" while also knowing full well that I didn't need to be [there] to also experience His full presence.[30]

Certainly, the leadership of Asbury University and Asbury Seminary, caring for and protecting the spiritual awakening in their midst from attempts to co-opt or besmirch it, knew that God's Spirit poured out on Gen Z students was not intended for them alone, but for any *wherever*, who would call upon his name. *Come* and *tarry*, yes, but by all means *"go* into all the world" to spread the good news of Jesus Christ. "It's my hope and prayer that it doesn't stop at Asbury," wrote Gracie Bradley of Eastern Kentucky University Baptist Campus Ministry, "but that it extends all over—we are called to be sent."[31]

There could be that temptation to tarry and to bask in the godly glow of the revival's joy unspeakable. Asbury Seminary Provost Gregg Okesson likened it to the account of Jesus's transfiguration when "His face shone like the sun, and his clothes became as white as the light" (Matt. 17:2b). Disciples Peter, James, and John wanted to stay put and build dwellings at the site of this high mountaintop experience. But Jesus would have none of that. There was kingdom work yet to be done in the valley. *Come* and *tarry*, yes, but by all means then *go*. On March 16–17, 2023, Dr. Okesson reported from meetings he was attending in Londrina, Brazil: "Everyone I meet here wants to hear a firsthand account of the Asbury Revival."[32]

On March 8, 2023, Pete Greig, pastor, author, vice president of the British charity Tearfund, and founder of the global 24–7 Prayer Movement, wrote a powerful essay on the spread of the Asbury Revival titled "The Popcorn Effect." In three weeks in February–March he traveled outside the United Kingdom to Kentucky, Oklahoma, Colorado, and Florida, and had conversations with people from Rwanda, Ukraine, Kenya, Nigeria, South Africa, New Zealand, Poland, Australia, Canada, India, China, Chile, and Brazil.

> Pretty much everyone I've met, and everywhere I've been, I've seen something I can only describe as: "The Asbury Effect."
>
> As a kid I loved making popcorn in the microwave. I learned to wait for the first promising pop, knowing that there would soon be another, then another, until there was that lovely machine gun volley of mini explosions. Heat those kernels to 170°C and 34% will pop. Wait another 10 degrees and 96% will be done. Those ten degrees make all the difference. The spiritual temperature seems to be rising, things are beginning to pop, as people everywhere—particularly students—hear about Asbury and begin seeking God's face with fresh expectancy in prayer. . . . I'm beginning to detect the temperature rising, a crescendo of tiny explosions, signs of our time and whispers of hope.[33]

Dr. Dennis Kinlaw, Asbury College president during the school's 1970 revival, used to say that when the story of revival is told, it is bound to reproduce itself.[34] Unlike any previous Asbury season of renewal, February 2023 attracted sympathetic Catholics. Deacon John Brannen of Lexington's Pax Christi Catholic Church told a reporter: "I'm glad some of our faithful have attended Asbury. Maybe they'll bring it back, and maybe that's been the Holy Spirit's plan all along. . . . If people fully understood what was going on (in the Eucharist), we would have another Asbury."[35]

There may never be a full human accounting of everyone who first came, tarried, and then left Wilmore refreshed, empowered, and commissioned by God's Holy Spirit to go forth with good news for others. But some tallies of those who came and then departed with new godly resolve have been attempted. By church affiliation the Asbury spiritual awakening drew at a minimum Anglicans, Baptists, Catholics, charismatics, Episcopalians, Methodists, Pentecostals, Presbyterians, and members of nondenominational churches. At least forty states were represented, as well as at least forty countries including Australia, Austria, Brazil, Canada, Chile, Columbia, Cuba, Finland, Guatemala, Haiti, India, Indonesia, Ireland, Italy, Japan, Kenya, Latvia, Malaysia, Mexico, Myanmar, New Zealand, Nicaragua, Nigeria, Norway, Paraguay, Peru, Poland, Portugal, Russia, Singapore, South Africa, South Korea, Spain, Thailand, Uganda, Ukraine, the United Kingdom, the United States, Zambia, and Zimbabwe.[36] Very significant from the perspective of Gen Zers is the fact that students from at least 279 colleges and universities were represented among the tens of thousands who made their way to worship in Wilmore. Included in this number were students from at least 114 state schools. (See appendix D.)[37]

The stress many participants in the Asbury Outpouring placed upon "radical unity," meaning no divisions in the body of Christ, manifested itself in various ways. Student body president Alison Perfater and *Collegian* editor Alexandra Presta both witnessed greater student unity in response to the outpouring, evidenced in the decline in campus cliques and the increase in forgiveness for past divisions.[38] As noted, this unity expressed itself in the diversity of denominations, states, countries, and colleges and universities in attendance. It was reflected as well in the revival's stress upon "every nation, tribe, people and language" (Rev. 7:9) being a part in the worship of God. (See "A Critique of the Critics," appendix A.)

One additional reflection of "radical unity" was the range of representatives of ecclesial and theological camps communing and worshipping together in harmony. Catholic attendance and commendation for the outpouring was fulsome and unique in Asbury's experience. Baptist participation and affirmation of the revival was also much in evidence. Widespread Wesleyan participation was no surprise, but Reformed presence was. Professor Rob Lim stressed this point, noting as an example, the attendance of Regent College Professor Bruce Hindmarsh. This Reformed theologian gave a positive critique of the Asbury Outpouring, noting in particular the broad participation and wide acceptance across denominational lines, unique in his study of revival movements.[39]

twelve

CONCLUSION OR COMMENCEMENT

Empowered to Forgive and Reconcile

From President Haynes to Dr. Coleman

[Revival was] unplanned and unexpected . . . the absolute absence of human leadership. [It] . . . occupies everybody and all our wakeful hours. . . . Unusual, profound conviction pervades the assembly. The entire chapel is an altar. . . . I haven't told half the story. It cannot be told in human words. I wish I could portray its grandeur, its glory, and its graciousness.

So wrote Asbury College President B. F. Haynes—not about 2023, but about 1905, the very revival that propelled E. Stanley Jones to missionary service in India and beyond.[1] What is fascinating is how well Haynes's description fits 2023 as well as 1905.

"Whatever this is or has become," wrote Professor Rich Manieri in the February 24 *Asbury Collegian*:

Let's remember that it began with a small group of students who lingered after chapel. This is pure, unplanned, organic. No big-name speakers or musicians, no pyrotechnics. . . . This is not a performance. It is, however, a chorus of forgiven sinners crying out in thanksgiving to an almighty God. It is, as Asbury President Kevin Brown called it, "a beautiful, historic moment of spiritual renewal."[2]

One Wilmore retiree is in a unique position to comprehend how historic 2023 is as a "moment of spiritual renewal." Dr. Robert Coleman has lived long enough to experience "one divine moment" three times. He was a student at Asbury during its 1950 revival that had a profound influence on the trajectory of his life. He then was on the faculty of Asbury Seminary during the 1970 revival, the account of which he shared with the world through his book, *One Divine Moment*. And by God's grace at age ninety-four he was also able to partake of the Asbury Outpouring of 2023.[3]

"When the Dust Settles"

In the midst of Asbury's spiritual renewal, student Anna Lowe wrote powerfully in the *Asbury Collegian* of what should be hoped for "When the Dust Settles." Her essay received a remarkable seventy-two online responses by the date I checked in March 2023. One was from Phoenix from Deb Ludden Weidenhamer, Asbury College class of 1987:

> What tremendous insight for our spiritual responsibility to look past the moment into eternity. I was 5 years old when I stood in the last row on top of the wood chapel seats in Hughes during the 1970 revival. Not fully understanding the moment, the fragrant smell in the air, physical tingling in my skin, and beautiful raised voices in worship is the memory that connects me to the Holy Spirit. "There's a sweet, sweet, spirit in this place" plays

the song of praise on repeat as I have needed Christ in the most desperate times during my life since that revival. So Anna, I pray that you will be branded forever by this revival as it only takes that one momentary touch by the Holy Spirit to last your lifetime.[4]

Like Anna Lowe, Asbury Seminary President Timothy Tennent came to reflect on the revival's lifetime legacy as well as its immediate blessing:

> This outpouring reveals that it has the same elements which are found in any authentic revival: people repenting of their sins; people being filled with the Holy Spirit; men and women finding reconciliation with God and their neighbor; people capturing a renewed love for Jesus, the gospel, and the Holy Scriptures. All of the above has been happening here day after day. . . . Someday we will look back on these days and thank God that he visited us in ways we will talk about for years to come. But what we are doggedly seeking is not lasting memories, but transformed lives long after the lights go out in Hughes Auditorium or Estes Chapel or all other places which are experiencing this work of grace.[5]

An Artifact of Amazing Grace

Readers may recall it was the afternoon of February 8, 2023, that President Kevin Brown and a small clutch of close advisors retreated to a ground-floor hallway of Hughes Auditorium. There they made a pivotal decision to allow students to continue worshipping through the night if they so chose. That was the launch of 372 hours throughout sixteen days of an uninterrupted season of spiritual renewal on the campuses of Asbury University and Asbury Seminary. Even in the revival's final days, when

Hughes Auditorium was closed to the public in the middle of the night for cleaning, worship teams in two-hour shifts chose to continue lifting their voices in praise to the Lord.

A wall of historical photographs line the hallway where President Brown and others made their commitment to support and protect what was happening upstairs. One photo of the 1928 groundbreaking ceremony for the construction of Hughes Auditorium includes founding President John Wesley Hughes, Asbury Seminary President Henry Clay Morrison, and other notables. One can count it as an extraordinary artifact of amazing grace if one is privy to a sad chapter in Asbury's institutional history. In January 1904 President Hughes transferred the assets of Asbury College, up to that point his legal possession, to its board of trustees. One fateful day before the year was out, President Hughes received a phone message in which he learned that he was being dismissed as president. It was shocking because the board's decision came to his attention by means of a phone call from Texas from the newly elected president, who in the end never showed up to accept the position.[6]

Dr. Hughes went on to found short-lived Kingswood College, Breckinridge County, Kentucky, and retired back to Wilmore in 1915, where he befriended and mentored college and seminary ministerial students. Reflecting on 1904, Hughes wrote in his autobiography how "dazed and dumbfounded, perplexed and grieved" he had been upon his dismissal. Nevertheless, in time he overcame his painful departure from Wilmore. According to Dr. Joseph Thacker's history of Asbury College, Hughes "never exhibited bitterness toward those who had removed him from the presidency, nor did he show any jealousy toward those who followed him in the presidency."[7]

Yes, the Asbury board chose to name the new auditorium after the school's founding president. And, yes, Henry Clay Morrison had nothing to do with Hughes's ouster twenty-five years prior. Still, to this writer that photo of the founding president and and H. C. Morrison, Asbury's subsequent twice-serving president, hanging on a ground-floor wall of Hughes Auditorium is an exemplar of forgiveness that the Holy Spirit granted John Wesley Hughes. Subsequently, upstairs in 1950, 1958, 1970, 2006, and now 2023, and in a host of other less-celebrated years, many an Asbury student—and visitor to campus—has received forgiveness from a merciful Savior and, like President Hughes, has been empowered to forgive and reconcile in turn. It is that spiritual transformation at that altar upstairs that has made for godly lives of obedience, sacrifice, and service that only heaven can count.

The Sad Shallowness of a Life Given Over to Self-Absorption

Fast-forward from the 1928 photograph to 2023, to five days prior to the February onset of the spiritual outpouring on the campus of Asbury University. President Kevin Brown spoke in chapel on "The Difficulty of Being True to Yourself." That February 3 he gave students a penetrating critique of the sad shallowness of a life given over to self-absorption. As an alternative, he proposed the hope and joy, whatever the circumstances, of a life given over to Christ instead. Here he spoke of the paradoxes of faith that so confound the world:

- "When we empty ourselves, we become whole."
- "In binding love we find freedom."
- "Real freedom is to give ourselves to others and to give ourselves to our Creator."

It is the plan of a loving Father in which being true to self is finding new life in Christ. For President Brown this truth is to be found in Scripture: "For we are God's masterpiece. He has created us anew in Christ Jesus, so we can do the good things he planned for us long ago" (Eph. 2:10 NLT).

With the benefit of hindsight, President Brown's chapel message Friday, February 3, 2023, appears to have unknowingly anticipated February 8. Through mercy and splendor, the Holy Spirit was about to work a new miracle of cleansing, starting in Hughes Auditorium—but through social media, rapidly spreading across a spiritually hungry nation and world. The president's closing prayer in that chapel, winter of 2023, was thanksgiving: "Thank You, Father, for this place."[8]

But lest Asbury should boast, the frequent spontaneous revivals bestowed upon Asbury have not stemmed from its being "holier than thou." No, just the opposite. The instances in which the Asbury community has fallen short of "holiness unto the Lord" has meant that startling visitations of the Holy Spirit have been required to send it to its knees to revive it, again and again, through repentance. By this means—and this means alone—is it possible to make a *fresh* start in pursuit of holiness. May this pursuit serve as a fitting commencement, rather than conclusion, to this account.

appendix a

A CRITIQUE OF THE CRITICS

"Too Much" or "Not Enough"

Historically, spiritual awakenings typically have attracted fringe elements that have given these movements a bad name. Even biblically sound preaching, if delivered in an unaccustomed manner, can raise objections from traditionalists. Many eighteenth-century Anglicans, for example, were scandalized by John Wesley's field preaching and the emotion that often accompanied the conversion of England's poor and heavy laden. It was so much the case that early Methodists came to be pejoratively typecast as "enthusiasts." The same is true for Asbury spiritual awakenings.

The literature and social media coverage of Asbury University's spiritual awakening in February 2023 is already vast. Doing a simple Google search of "Asbury Revival" underscores the point. At first, positive social media predominated, with stress on the winsome nature of unplanned, weeks-long worship launched by university students. But in due course, negative critiques of the revival began to appear, especially, it seemed, on YouTube. Those with reservations have argued that spiritual renewal at Asbury was suspect because it was "too much" of something or it was "not enough" of something else. And in keeping with the curse of

America's deepening culture war divide, some on the left said it was too much of the majority culture,[1] while Christian nationalists on the right hoped to enlist it for their political agenda.[2] For some it was too emotional, while for others it was not emotional enough. Was it really spontaneous, or did it just appear to be? Some theological fundamentalists felt women were too much in evidence preaching and teaching, while some theological progressives did not observe enough stress upon racial reconciliation and social justice. Some of Pentecostal and charismatic persuasion desired more signs and wonders, more dramatic physical healings, and more glossolalia. Others falsely claimed there was no preaching. Finally, the self-servers did not enjoy opportunities for their ministry and their "brand" to lead, to shine, and thereby extend their following on social media.

Initial Hesitation for Some

Evaluations of all these reservations will be forthcoming. But first, instances of uncertainty within the Asbury community itself as to how to process spontaneous revival also deserve consideration. On February 21, 2023, I asked a student of my acquaintance what the highlight of the revival was for her. We were standing outside Hughes Auditorium in front of Kinlaw Library, named for Asbury's president who forever christened the 1970 Asbury Revival "one divine moment." This student said the highlight for her was the first few days when the spiritual awakening was predominately an Asbury student renewal.[3] Always gracious, what she did not say was that as word spread on social media a number of students, faculty, and staff—not to mention Wilmore citizens—felt overwhelmed by the press of humanity that engulfed Hughes, the campus, and the community. Some did not know what to make of it. One faculty member shared with this writer, "I don't come from a revivalist culture. What is this?"

Some professors were supportive, but still processing the unexpected. Some of their students also found navigating the revival challenging. Were they spiritually lacking if they were not caught up in through-the-night worship?

Another student I have known for years confided that, at first, she "stiff-armed" the awakening. Though from a strong Christian home, she had never witnessed what people were calling spontaneous revival. She was confused and hesitant, but willing to be open. On February 8 she was in Hughes, 2:00 p.m. until 11:00 p.m., trying to discern, "Is this from you, God?" Then again she tarried in Hughes for extended hours on February 9. Especially painful for this student was seeing one of her classmates leading worship who had hurt her deeply the previous year. Then a "big thing" happened. "This person came up to me and asked for forgiveness. I did forgive, and a weight was lifted off."

Still pondering it all, this student shared that some of her friends were in Hughes all night long, while others were "really hesitant to be in Hughes—still trying to figure it out." She saw some students blessed, some bothered, many inconvenienced: "all across the spectrum" in terms of reaction. To the good, she knew students who through prayer had been freed from "the burden of comparison," a major source of anxiety for Gen Zers. In her theology class her professor led discussions on the revival for a whole week, and that had been "super helpful."[4]

My serious, searching student interlocutor, sometimes baffled, sometimes blessed, asked a key question: "Is this from you, God?" It speaks to the skepticism Asbury's 2023 spiritual awakening evoked from representatives of American secular society and also from some staid Christians uncomfortable with revivalism, Holy Spirit religion, and—God forbid—the saved and sanctified showing emotion. At the other extreme were those who complained that Asbury's spiritual renewal was not emotional and dramatic enough to be counted as a "real" revival.

Marks of Authenticity: Unplanned

What then, in the face of its critics, left and right, are marks of authenticity that Asbury's defenders might enlist to affirm February 2023 as a genuine work of spiritual renewal? For one, by all accounts this Asbury awakening was unplanned. Asbury Seminary staff member Kelly Bixler walked the university campus and then called to mind: "This is an educational institution that currently has classes going on and mid-terms are looming! Did I mention it's almost mid-terms (that's incredibly poor planning if this were manufactured or preplanned)?!!" President Kevin Brown called the campus's efforts accommodation rather than orchestration.[5] One participant, and not of the Asbury tribe, told a *Washington Post* reporter onsite: "You can't tell a bunch of college students that we're going to pray together all night and share our secrets. You can't plan that or engineer that."[6] Another observer from another institution was of the same opinion: "For what it's worth, it's my initial evaluation that this is the real deal. None of the hallmarks of manufactured revival are present."[7] Asbury Seminary's Ben Witherington made the same point:

> Yes, this has happened before at Asbury . . . but neither in the past nor on this occasion was this something planned. You can't really plan for when God may choose to show up and visit in a palpable way. Trust me, many were as startled by this awakening as was Mary when Gabriel suddenly appeared to that teenage girl and said—by the way you're about to be miraculously pregnant and become the mother of the Messiah.[8]

Biblical scholar Craig Keener recalls:

> While years of prayer preceded this experience at Asbury, the timing and manner took us all by surprise. Actually, I will confess . . . in my arrogance I had sometimes hoped

that maybe revival would happen when *I* preached in chapel or taught *my* New Testament class at the seminary. But God in his gracious wisdom did it in a way that nobody else could even try to take credit for. The outpouring was God's action, His initiative. His Spirit fell as students were caught up in worship.[9]

Some critics have argued that Asbury's previous unplanned and protracted revivals have almost all come in February (1905, 1908, 1921, 1950, 1970, 2006, and 2023), with the other two in March (1958 and 1992)—so they must be contrived.[10] Asbury students and graduates who in recent years have been praying for a fresh anointing of the Holy Spirit in their lives and on their campus certainly recall or have been told of the 1970 and other extended Asbury revivals. And perhaps they prayed with greater earnestness through gray winter months. But detractors must know that Christians believe God answers prayer. And from a believer's perspective, if God responds in a February or March to especially heartfelt prayers for a fresh visitation of the Holy Spirit, that timing makes an outpouring of his grace no less genuine. Writes Professor Keener: "One night when I was teaching in Indonesia, I dreamed that the most important insight from the decade of work in my four-volume Acts commentary was how often the outpouring of the Spirit follows prayer."[11] In King James Version language, "The effectual fervent prayer of a righteous man availeth much" (James 5:16b).

Marks of Authenticity: Contrition and Confession

Another hallmark of a genuine outpouring of God's Spirit are testimonies of confession, repentance, and forgiveness; and these in public are not the natural pastime of typically proud, self-absorbed humankind. Based on their reading of the book of Acts some critics have contended that not enough conversions were in evidence to call Asbury's sixteen days of services a "real" revival. Professor Craig Keener discounts this charge:

> Some outpourings of the Spirit in history led immediately and directly to conversions, and some want to impose that template on any outpouring. While many were converted on the Day of Pentecost, however, it is *not* stated for the next outpouring, in Acts 4, or the next in Acts 8, or most others in Acts. Yet it did happen at Asbury. . . . But the key purpose of outpourings of the Spirit in Acts was to empower God's people for mission (Acts 1:8), and that has characterized all the Asbury outpourings so far. In this one many, touched by God's holiness, consecrated their lives to His service.[12]

As for conversions, Keener did not know if anyone did—or could—keep an accurate tally, but conservatively he believed it was in the hundreds.[13] Dr. Mark Troyer, Asbury University vice president of institutional advancement, estimated Hughes Auditorium saw four hundred to five hundred first-time commitments and thousands of pilgrims rededicating their lives to Christ.[14] And this is before taking into account the untold spiritual fruit from the multiple overflow venues of Asbury Seminary, Wilmore churches, and even the spiritual blessings on Asbury's semicircle lawn where thousands not able to enter Hughes worshipped with the aid of simulcast screens.

The student-run *Asbury Collegian* was full of accounts of contrition and a new or deeper life in Christ throughout February 2023, including some articles already quoted. About fifty Asbury students attend Porter Memorial Baptist Church in Lexington. On Facebook lead pastor Nick Sandfur shared: "I have heard their stories and know that God moved in many hearts. . . . I do believe that God showed up in a powerful way at Asbury."[15] Speaking of all dimensions of revival worship, Kenny Rager of the Kentucky

Baptist Convention wrote: "I went. I felt the Lord's presence. I saw people worship. I saw people praying. I heard the Word preached. I met new brothers and sisters in the Lord, and I felt the Lord speak to me about some issues."[16]

The Lord did speak to many about all manner of issues, Asbury's heavily burdened Gen Z students not the least. One more proof of a "real" revival was the eight-fold drop in university counseling appointments in the months after February 2023.[17] Wrote Asbury Seminary's Dr. Lawson Stone: "It's confession, repentance, reconciliation, restitution, and renewed love. People try to get control of it and the sweet water just runs through their fingers."[18]

Marks of Authenticity: The Super Bowl Could Not Compete

Another proof of authenticity? The Super Bowl could not compete with the Asbury Revival the night of February 12: "One of our culture's most ubiquitous communal experiences did not even put a dent in the attendance at Hughes Auditorium," noted Northern Seminary Professor Thomas Lyons.[19] Asbury student Mia Lush told local NBC affiliate LEX 18: "People are coming from all over, and they don't want to be anywhere else but here. Like, I'm a big Eagles fan, and I didn't even watch the Super Bowl. I've been able to surrender things that I didn't even know I would be able to surrender."[20]

Marks of Authenticity: From Hate to Love

Evidences of love and unity of spirit replacing division are also profound markers of spiritual revitalization. The reporting of *Asbury Collegian* editor Alexandra Presta struck this writer as outstanding throughout February 2023, including this reflection on Love with a capital L:

Now I can see that we are acting differently. We're taking care of each other, constantly checking in if we're eating and sleeping enough. We're processing hardships together and praying bold prayers for healing, and prayers against any and all spiritual warfare. Because as Paul says in 1 Corinthians, Love "always protects, always trusts, always hopes, always perseveres" (13:7).[21]

Asbury junior Kyla Powell said as much:

This weekend [February 10–12] has shown a glimpse of what it looks like when we put aside our differences and come together to be in the presence of God. What can happen when the body of Christ is united in Love and not divided by irrelevant things is beautiful.[22]

On the subject of love, Asbury student body president Alison Perfater was blunt, no-nonsense, and on target: "I know this campus very well. It's small. And I know exactly which students on this campus hate each other. Those are the people I have seen praying together, singing together, hugging, crying. . . . It's been totally life-changing."[23]

Harold Rainwater, founding director of the Asbury University Equine Center and Wilmore mayor, also observed a turn for the better among his students in the wake of the February spiritual awakening: better class attendance, stronger commitment to the program, no "senior fatigue" among graduating equine majors, and a bonanza of considerate behavior in student interactions. The mayor had moist eyes in describing these signposts of spiritual renewal. He shared one particularly memorable instance of post-revival tenderheartedness. Given $100 by the Equine Center to "pay it forward," one enterprising and creative student painstakingly taught her mount to "paint" by giving rewards when her horse held a brush in its teeth and dabbed, at random, on a proffered "canvas." Five of these "masterpieces" sold for $200 each for a collective donation to charity of $1,000.[24]

Asbury Seminary Professor Ben Witherington did not see the February 2023 spiritual renewal as "contrived," nor "fully explained by sociological studies." Rather, one of the markers of its authenticity, he contends, is "holiness—the sanctifying of the Christian life, including the manifestation of the fruit of the Spirit—love, joy, peace, patience, kindness, self-control and much more. . . . Hopefully, it will touch many, many lives and make them all better, after a terrible cultural season of bitterness, cynicism, hate, gun violence, pandemic, distrust, and worse. Frankly, the whole country needs revival. I pray it can be sparked by what is happening here."[25]

Markers of Authenticity: A Compulsion to Share Good News

Business Professor Rob Lim related that he had students, spiritually awakened in February, who could not contain their joy. He described it as a compulsion many had to share the love of God wherever. "No one told them to do it." Before the end of the semester, without faculty or others urging or suggesting, they simply took the initiative in March and April to travel to colleges and churches to give bold witness. In two words: God led. Professor Lim saw it as a sign of a genuine work of God in Asbury's students.[26]

Markers of Authenticity: "A Long Obedience in the Same Direction"

Another marker of an authentic outpouring of the Holy Spirit, which can only be fully reckoned over time, will be the extent to which the newly redeemed and the newly sanctified express their faith in terms of "a long obedience in the same direction," to quote theologian Eugene Peterson.[27] Will those quickened by the

Spirit never return to "casual prayers" and "domesticated faith"? (Timothy Tennent). Will its beneficiaries have the fortitude to "withstand cultural pressures to conform and compromise?" (Steve Seamands). For decades to come will the renewed be "engaged to labor with earnestness and activity in His service, and made willing to go through all difficulties for His sake?" (Jonathan Edwards).[28]

Over the long haul there will need to be proof on many levels of love for all. Such evidence will be acting upon love for the lost (evangelism and missions), acting upon love for the poor (compassionate ministry to lift up the marginalized), and acting upon love toward those of every nation, tribe, people, and tongue (advocacy for justice for all and racial reconciliation). Writes Professor Nicholson:

> The Holy Spirit has graciously sent gentle flood waters to revive us, reshape us, and empower us for the work ahead. . . . This flood we are experiencing today is meant to revive us for a purpose—to share the joy and the love of God with those living in a dark world. As this revival has been occurring, we have simultaneously watched tens of thousands of dead being pulled from the rubble after the earthquake in Turkey and Syria. We have witnessed several more mass shootings, including one on the campus of Michigan State University. We continue to see famine and poverty, addiction and despair, racism and sexism, abuse and ailments across the world and in our homes. We need this refreshing of the Spirit more than ever as a testimony that God has not abandoned this dark world. . . . [But] if we keep this refreshing Spirit to ourselves, then we have missed the point.[29]

The Asbury institutions have historically placed great emphasis upon evangelism and missions, and the biblical imperative to reach the lost is still demonstrably part of their DNA. Concern for the poor, likewise, has been and remains a felt obligation of

Asbury administrators and faculties. The university's social work major, the seminary's long-standing emphasis upon inner-city ministry, and both institutions' long and intimate association with the Salvation Army underscore the point.

Coming to Terms with Race

Unfortunately, the track record of the two schools on racial reconciliation has been mixed, though strides forward are being made. Both the university and the seminary were late in integrating their student bodies, and the faculty and student racial composition is still less than ideal for institutions that historically have striven to promote "the whole Bible for the whole world." Still, they are moving in the right direction. The seminary, with its ample funding for international students, now underwrites a substantial enrollment from Africa, Asia, and Latin America. And as the university is able to increase its endowment, the will is there to increase its minority faculty and student representation.

Asbury University's February 2023 spiritual renewal is itself an illustration of forward movement in overcoming racial divides. Most of its gospel choir members who sang in the chapel service on February 8 are African American with Africans and Latinos as well. Three African American singers, along with the altar prayers of Asbury undergrads who remained after chapel, were the mustard seeds that grew into the largest and longest-lasting spontaneous renewal in the university's history (over 370 hours).[30] Others of color included chapel worship leaders Georges Dumaine, Charity Johnson, Lena Marlowe, and Sarah Cawley, and gospel choir director and pianist Benjamin Black.[31] For Chaplain Haseloff the gospel choir "was part of the impact of this outpouring . . . from the beginning," reflecting "the multiethnic composition of God's Kingdom."[32]

Professor Craig Keener and his wife, Medine, a native of the Republic of the Congo, had been praying for years for a fresh visitation of the Holy Spirit at Asbury. In a dream well before February 2023, Dr. Keener had a vision of a revival in Hughes Auditorium:

> We were going out into the community to welcome people. As I knocked on one door, an older African American man asked if he would be welcome. "That," I answered in the dream, "will be how we know if it's a true revival." But happily, God fixed that from the beginning, since many of the members of the gospel choir where the outpouring started are Black. Racial unity was one of the outpouring's central foundations.

Keener continued:

> In the final analysis, people met Jesus deeply here. We thank God for the obedience of . . . the gospel choir, who overwhelmed by the Spirit, just kept worshipping. By the time they were done, tens of thousands of other people had joined in worshipping the same Lord.[33]

Gospel choir director Benjamin Black and his wife, chapel coordinator Madeline Black, have had a heart for multiethnic worship leaders—and worshippers—for well before Asbury's February 2023 outpouring. In forming worship teams for the Hughes platform, Madeline was proactive in striving for "radical unity" for Asbury's praise to God. In her planning, representation from every nation, tribe, people, and tongue was "a pillar of everyday thinking to honor the Lord," with a majority of worship teams being ethnically diverse. Malaysian Australian faculty member and Hughes platform speaker Rob Lim has estimated that 30 to 40 percent of worship team members were persons of color during the outpouring.[34]

The Woodlands Methodist Church near Houston provided a team of experienced worship leaders to supplement the ministry of "Madeline and company" who were nearing exhaustion after a week of nonstop worship in Hughes Auditorium. Woodlands Associate Pastor Mark Swayze found it "fascinating to watch" Madeline mix and match in worship team formation. Highly complimentary of this twenty-four-year-old fulfilling a pressure-packed role, he respected her willingness to gently chide and correct if worship team rotations began to drift in too racially homogenous a direction.[35]

Haitian American worship leader Georges Dumaine on occasion was disappointed when the platform party fell short of the goal of radical ethnic unity. Mary—she prefers a pseudonym because of her ministry in a restricted-access country—was the widely respected leader of a behind-the-scenes program of prayers of consecration for the multitude of worship teams. Also a champion of radical ethnic unity in worship leadership, she, too, could be saddened when platform musicians and speakers were too regularly Caucasian. At the same time, Mary believes it is of "prophetic significance" for Asbury moving forward that during the outpouring several worship and prayer leaders were members of interracial marriages: Ben and Madeline Black, Georges and Katie Dumaine, and Mary and her African husband.[36]

On the seminary side, students of color from the global south were much in evidence and among the most energetic supporters of Asbury's spiritual awakening.[37] For five years every Friday afternoon in Estes Chapel, Dr. Steve Seamands was involved with a group initiated by three seminary students (Matthew Hulbert, Davie Ferraro, and Rob Lim), praying for revival. As a rule, half of this group consisted of international students. Professor Lim even recalled having a dream centered on the university chapel in which the name of the auditorium was spelled Hues instead of Hughes.[38] Diane Ury drove nine hours from Raleigh, North Carolina, to serve as an altar counselor for several of the last days, ministering both in Hughes Auditorium and McKenna Chapel. After many hours serving indoors, this Salvation Army pastor stepped outside and was amazed to see thousands of pilgrims on the semicircle lawn. It was a sea of races, she recalled: "about 50 percent Caucasian and 50 percent African American, Asian, and Latino."[39]

Ushering the last three days of the revival, I also was struck by the multi-hues of worshippers, more ethnically diverse than I have ever seen Hughes Auditorium—Latino, Asian, and African American youth and families were much in evidence. Professor Rob Lim, as well, saw the last nights of services in Hughes as racially diverse, even a majority non-Caucasian. From the platform he recalled seeing "two-three rows" each of Asian Indians, African Americans, Africans, and Hispanics.[40] Asbury University would be delighted if this multiracial representation on campus would translate into increased admissions of students of color. As Asbury University student Dorcus Lara from Uganda put it: "One of the recurring themes in the revival . . . is the diversity of the kingdom of God. We should be a replication of what heaven is like. . . . Heaven is for different languages, races, and ethnicities coming together to worship God."[41]

Wilmore, as well, is making some progress in casting off a Dixie disposition, as was underscored by many cases of inter-racial hospitality in February 2023. (Historians frequently note that, paradoxically, border-state Kentucky in effect "joined" the Confederacy *after* the Civil War.)[42] Unfortunately, Jim Crow discrimination and segregation held sway in Wilmore and Kentucky way too long.

Hospitality on the House

In response to the explosive spread of news of Asbury's 2023 revival, the university designated a human resources staffer to field the flood of calls from people wanting to come worship in Hughes. (A new campus switchboard operator happened to start work on February 8 and was completely overwhelmed.)[43] In tandem, a "hospitality team" mushroomed almost overnight. It came to the rescue of an African American family from Columbus, Ohio, that needed housing on short notice. Ashley Grant and her husband, both ministers, worshiped in Hughes, accompanied by their three children, ages six, two, and six weeks.[44] (This usher had never seen as many children and baby carriages in Hughes Auditorium as during this revival.)

The *Washington Post*'s onsite African American reporter, Amber Ferguson, related the following saga of the Grant family:

> "We wanted to be there, to have our presence there, to have Gen Z basically know that we are standing with [them]," said Grant . . . [who] saw miracles and healing take place and heard testimonies of people talking about their depression and suicidal thoughts during the revival. However, what struck her most was the hospitality. A group of college students had coloring books and crayons and played with her older sons for hours, she recalled. "They had food and beverages. You didn't have to leave that building for any supplies."

On their fourth night attending, it was too late in the day for the couple to drive home. The hospitality team set the family up in an upstairs apartment of a couple who lived two minutes from the university. "We think that revival is only preaching of the Gospel and crying out. But actually, it's when the love of God is being displayed," Grant said.

"Here we are, a young Black couple, and there's an older White couple offering us their home to sleep in for however long we want, and they made us feel like we were at home," she said. "They didn't know us." "The only thing they have in common [wrote reporter Ferguson] is the man, Christ Jesus. That's when you know that something has taken place."[45]

The Priority of Multicultural Spiritual Unity

Wholehearted affirmation of spiritual unity as one of the hallmarks of the outpouring was a singular achievement of Asbury University and Asbury Seminary leadership. As the administrations understood the leading of the Holy Spirit, they saw themselves as both witnesses and guardians of an all-encompassing unity that was welcoming to all denominations, all ages, all classes, all nations, and all races. In staving off contrary agendas their efforts focused on protecting God's soul work in their midst from politics of all persuasions, including Christian nationalism which was seen as undermining believers' first allegiance to God.

To be held at more than arms' length were certain revivalists who mix faith with a racially tinged culture war combativeness to the detriment of any genuine outpouring of the Holy Spirit. Protecting the revival from such was a determined goal of the university and the seminary. One indication that they largely succeeded may be deduced from the dramatic influx of pilgrims to Asbury who represented every "nation, tribe, people and language" (Rev. 7:9). The platform in Hughes visibly underscored the point not only through the gospel choir and worship teams but with Korean American mission professor Sam Kim leading prayers for the nations, Asian Indian Assistant Vice President of Intercultural Affairs Esther Jadhav teaching, Malaysian Australian Professor of Business Rob Lim preaching, and the last week of services when the nations literally came to Wilmore.[46]

Just as the largely African American gospel choir was one "bookend" that helped launch Asbury's spiritual renewal, so too a

Latin world "bookend" was much in evidence in its closing days.
On Facebook, Vice President Sarah Baldwin posted:

> I don't want to forget the Latino family—grandpa, dad,
> uncle, kids, mama—who when they made it into Hughes
> after what must have been a wait of hours—didn't even
> go to their seats. They went immediately to the altar and
> collapsed in front of it. We saw this again and again. I
> [also] want to remember the family who drove 30 hours
> each way from Mexico for someone to pray over their
> baby for healing.[47]

Prayer counselor training leader and former missionary to
Brazil Bud Simon connected with forty Brazilians on the semicircle where they knelt around a flag of their nation, praying for
a fresh work of God among their countrymen.[48] They made their
presence known in Hughes as well. Dr. Baldwin recalls: "Who can
forget the Brazilians! They showed up! Their passionate prayers
for their country! All the Brazilian flags (although graciously put
away when we asked—just too many people for all the flags)."[49] The
second weekend of the outpouring Haitian American Georges
Dumaine called on the peoples of the world, much in evidence, to
sing in their native tongues.[50]

The Better Angels of Wesleyan Persuasion

The better angels of Wesleyan persuasion from John and Charles
Wesley to the current presidents of Asbury University and Asbury
Seminary have stood in opposition to any semblance of Christian
faith devoid of wholehearted love and respect for every soul created
in God's image. John Wesley is well-known for his unequivocal
opposition to slavery. Francis Asbury, commissioned by Wesley
for missionary service in America, whose equestrian statue stands

adjacent to the university and seminary campuses that bear his name, likewise strongly condemned one person's "ownership" of another. And Asbury University's revered graduate, missionary to India, E. Stanley Jones, championed a multicultural Christian faith in his classic *Christ of the Indian Road.*[51]

Still, it must be noted that while Wesley and Asbury opposed slavery and Jones opposed segregation, Methodists in the American South defended first slavery and later, in the main, Jim Crow racial discrimination and segregation. Self-emancipated Frederick Douglass, ardent champion of the abolition of slavery, personally experienced the worst imaginable example of revivalism unworthy of the name: "In August, 1832, my master attended a Methodist camp-meeting . . . and there experienced religion. . . . If it had any effect on his character, it made him more cruel and hateful in all his ways; for I believe him to have been a much worse man after his conversion than before."[52]

Such was a betrayal of the heart of compassion of Christian faith properly understood and practiced. Fortunately—and amazingly—his "converted" master's bogus religiosity did not cause Douglass to renounce faith in the Almighty. Instead, his conviction was to place his faith in the "Christianity of Christ" that was a balm to the oppressed and heavy-laden.[53]

As regards social holiness, Asbury's flock, and indeed all Christ-followers in America, can draw inspiration from the example of revival-minded northern Christians prior to the Civil War. They not only preached and practiced all manner of compassionate ministries, many also were ardent, activist opponents of slavery on religious grounds. The case is ably laid out in *Revivalism and Social Reform: American Protestantism on the Eve of the Civil War* by Johns Hopkins University's Timothy L. Smith, respected academic and ordained Nazarene pastor.[54] Back in the 1990s Asbury College President Dennis Kinlaw was pleased to have Dr. Smith preach in Hughes Auditorium.

Defenders of Asbury's Spiritual Outpouring

Various voices sympathetic to the Asbury spiritual awakening have countered a host of additional criticisms of February 2023. Asbury Seminary Professor Craig Keener noted: "Some who love high view counts have jumped on an anti-revival bandwagon."[55] Also to the point, Dr. Keener's Asbury Seminary colleague, Old Testament Professor Lawson Stone, notes:

> Various groups have tried to force our revivals into different templates, their templates, whether it's "Signs and Wonders" or "Last Days Great Awakening" notions . . . but they always peter out. But the transparency, openness, the spirit of repentance and reconciliation . . . that is self-sustaining.[56]

Some of the most thoughtful reflections on the Asbury Outpouring of 2023 have come from Dr. Tim Beougher, Southern Seminary professor and pastor of Louisville's West Broadway Baptist Church, perhaps in part because he played a leadership role during Wheaton College's spontaneous revival of 1995:

> A word of exhortation to all who journey to Wilmore. In Luke 7 we read the account of a woman washing Jesus' feet with her tears and anointing them with perfume. The Pharisee who was there was indignant at what he saw as a waste of valuable perfume—in his eyes. Jesus wasn't worth such extravagant worship. This passage reminds us that in every worship setting there will be three groups: the one being worshipped (the Lord), the worshippers, and spectators. How can you tell if you are a spectator and not a worshipper: Because you will be critical of how other people are worshipping, without realizing you aren't worshipping at all! For years my

prayer when I enter a sanctuary has been, "Lord, help me today to be a worshipper and not a spectator." I whispered that prayer as I entered Hughes this afternoon, and God graciously answered. I had sweet fellowship with my Savior, surrounded by hundreds of others doing the same. . . .

One final caution—throughout the history of revivals, critics have pointed to some type of "excess" accompanying a revival and tried to argue that "excess" discredited the entire revival movement and meant it wasn't truly a work of God. Jonathan Edwards answered that criticism during the First Great Awakening by using a helpful phrase: "in the main." What is at the heart of the movement? What is happening "in the main?" There will always be "excess" on the fringe due to overly excited and not yet completely sanctified human beings and/or to Satanic opposition, but what is taking place "in the main?" That is a helpful grid as we evaluate movements like that taking place now at Asbury.[57]

In an office interview Asbury University Chaplain Greg Haseloff voiced a similar sentiment: "The middle was so important that we could tolerate a whole lot on the side."[58]

Craig Keener's Critique

Perhaps the most comprehensive commentary to date answering charges against the Asbury awakening of February 2023 comes from Asbury Seminary Professor Craig Keener in a blog post. A sampling of some of the specific criticisms he refutes include the following:

• The Bible says nothing about outpourings of the Spirit: False. Read Acts.

- The Bible is against expressing emotion: False. Read Psalms. Healings, conversions, and consecration for mission . . . happened here. Falling down and shaking, not so much. If there's been any recent revival more tame evangelicals could be comfortable with, it should be this one. If someone can't stomach what happened here, they're probably not up for much of any outpouring of the Spirit.
- The revival has political associations: False. . . . I've heard no talk of politics and certainly not of political parties.
- The revival is about Christian nationalism: False. I don't know everyone on either campus, but everyone I do know here who has heard of Christian nationalism rejects it.
- The revival is racially exclusive: False. The worship team and leadership team are ethnically diverse, and the revival started from the university gospel choir's singing (and prayer).
- The revival is denominationally exclusive: False. It is a beautiful display of interdenominational unity.
- It's Pentecostal or charismatic. . . . False, on the whole. The school's heritage is Wesleyan. It's not anti-Pentecostal or anti-charismatic, so Pentecostals and charismatics attend, teach, work, and visit here like Christians from other traditions. But the focus lies elsewhere, and we are all getting along nicely. (I say this as a charismatic prof at the seminary across the street.)[59]

What troubled Dr. Keener more than any other criticism of the Asbury awakening was that proffered by a West Coast pastor, radio broadcaster, author, and blogger:

1. He has suggested that [a widely disgraced] Todd Bentley being present should discredit the revival.
    Response: Whatever Todd Bentley came *intending* to do, he was *not* allowed to minister on the university campus and was indeed required to *leave* it.

2. He claims that "Queer students have been leading worship"; "Revivals are not led by homosexuals."[60]

Because the LGBTQ lifestyle is increasingly such a major source of division in churches, Professor Keener's carefully nuanced response deserves a full hearing:

> The university prohibits sexual activity outside hetero-sexual marriage as stated explicitly and publicly online: "Sexual immorality (including adultery, same-sex behavior and premarital sexual intimacy). These behaviors are expressly prohibited in Scripture. Offenses in this area are almost certain to result in separation from the University for a period of time" (https://www.asbury.edu/life/resources/handbook-community-life/commitments/morality/). A student *known* to engage in such activity would not be allowed to lead worship, nor would they be allowed to remain a student. The leader I consulted knows of no one leading worship who is sexually active outside of marriage, of any sexual orientation. . . . The critic's source for the claim is a post from someone who calls himself a "gay seminarian," apparently writing about another "gay seminarian." Both who use the expression, however, use it to describe same-sex attraction, not sexual behavior. Whatever we may think of the label, they both describe themselves even more explicitly as *celibate*. Confessing sin differs from boasting in it, and confessing temptation differs from confessing sin. Jesus said that a person can sin even by desiring someone else sexually. But temptation is not the same thing as sin. Any hetero-sexual who has ever lusted has no room to throw stones at somebody whose sphere of temptation is same-sex. If we want to condemn people for where their temptations lie, we all stand condemned before a holy God. Someone

who condemns people for temptations, despite battling (or worse, indulging) temptations of their own, fits the biblical designation of a hypocrite. . . . God is at work at Asbury University, as he is in many other places, and we should celebrate his work. . . . Shouldn't all Jesus's followers celebrate that, whatever their other disagreements, and wherever they are? At the least, however, Jesus's followers should not promote falsehoods.[61]

The Work of God "In the Main"

In the last analysis, it is safe to say that those in sympathy with the Asbury Revival understand that unfounded charges and confirmed excesses on the margins pale before the cleansing work of the Holy Spirit in February 2023. Even in the book of Acts not everyone in the vicinity of the Holy Spirit's blessing had pure motives (5:1–2; 8:18–19).[62] The university administration naturally had less ability to superintend and protect the revival on the campus semicircle lawn—with its thousands—than it did in Hughes Auditorium. Lawson Stone was one who observed some excesses outside. One "harangue" on the lawn struck him as the opposite of the authentic blessing he and so many others were experiencing:

> The outpouring was peaceful. He was screaming.
> The outpouring was gentle. He was harsh.
> The outpouring didn't involve prodding or pushing. He was demanding a response.
> The outpouring was humble. He was angry.
> The outpouring did not center on a personality. The guy was all about himself.
> The outpouring was about JESUS. This guy was all about . . . "the revival."

It's so sad when the voices that want to perpetuate the revival (a good thing!) embody the exact opposite of everything that made the outpouring so wonderful.[63]

Still, contrary characters in Acts or on occasion on Asbury's semicircle cannot take away from the Spirit's work of grace in many lives. As Dr. Tim Beougher urged, it is worth recalling that the First Great Awakening's Jonathan Edwards stressed the importance of focusing on the fruits of revival "in the main."[64] He recognized that fringe elements would always be attracted to and attempt to co-opt or disparage genuine outpourings of God's grace. But such efforts on the margins should not be permitted to discredit the demonstrably changed hearts and minds newly empowered by God for lives of integrity, charity, justice, and service in his kingdom.

The Response of Asbury's Presidents to Criticism: Mostly Silence, Then an Apologia

Detractors will always be in evidence to malign and minimize extraordinary seasons of spiritual revitalization, finding them wanting for a host of reasons, as previously detailed. Thankfully, as noted, the revival did find its defenders who countered inaccurate reporting. In addition to Asbury faculty, those providing helpful critiques of the critics included quite a few with no ties to the Asbury institutions. In contrast, how did the leadership at Asbury University and Asbury Seminary react to the criticisms that the revival was not "right" in one way or another? At the time, mostly in silence. They wanted students to remain in the forefront, as they had been from the first inklings of revival on February 8, 2023. And responses to negative judgments from Asbury's university and seminary presidents might have detracted from the work of the Holy Spirit among Gen Z youth seeking redemption, relief, and consolation.

During the sixteen days of spiritual renewal, it is interesting to note how few official public communiqués were released by President Kevin Brown (three in print February 14, 16, and 24, and one in person in Hughes February 19) and by Asbury Seminary President Timothy Tennent (one on February 14).[65] There is much they justly could have said to defend the revival, but they both remained in the background for the most part. Between February 8 and 23 Asbury's presidents also gave relatively few media interviews in response to a phenomenon that garnered national and international attention. Instead of answering critics their preference was to let the repentance and renewal of students and pilgrims from near and far speak to the authenticity of God's outpouring of his Holy Spirit in little Wilmore, February 2023.

Now that "the dust has settled" a bit, to borrow from student Anna Lowe's *Collegian* article, President Brown addressed two questions dealing with criticism this author posed.

1. Did you consciously decide not to respond to negative critiques or were you just too busy to deal with them?

Entertaining criticisms—especially from non-proximate skeptics—is unlikely to be a fruitful exercise.

I should mention, I also recognized that there are many Christians or ex-Christians who have been the recipients of malformed or deformed expressions of religiosity or the Christian faith . . . or experienced an environment where attempts to re-create or manufacture a revival led to emotional or spiritual abuse. I know that is real for many people, so I understand skepticism when they see what occurred at Asbury. However, my heart was deeply moved when some of those very skeptics came to campus and experienced something very different. Something good, beautiful, powerful, right, transcendent, and true.

2. Are there any criticisms you would want to address now?

I actually have not spent a lot of time scanning various thoughts and criticisms. However, one thing I have encountered with frequency is whether what happened is truly a revival and variations of this question (i.e., we should be skeptical of what to call this, "this was planned," "this is just emotionalism," etc. etc.). I understand these questions. But as it relates to the compulsion over what to call this, I would simply offer the following: If one of my kids came home and told me that they had abandoned their previous schedule and sat at an altar of prayer for hours, prayed for repentance/forgiveness, made new life-altering commitments, worshipped the Lord, prayed with others, testified to God's goodness, and concluded by saying, "God really revived my heart." . . . Would it not be odd for my first response to be, "Well, are you sure it was a true 'revival'?" or "Are you sure God really did something for you? Maybe we should wait several months and see." It is not as if those questions are irrelevant or unimportant, but my first response would be deep gratitude and thankfulness.

President Brown prepared a more formal revival apologia for a video, part of which may serve as a fitting conclusion for a critique of the critics.

During the outpouring, there was a great deal of news and social media commentary seeking to describe what was occurring. Many wanted to name what was unfolding before the world's eyes. Was this a revival? A renewal? An outpouring? An awakening? What was the correct description of what was occurring? What was the most philosophically or theologically appropriate vocabulary to associate with what we witnessed before our eyes?

As I reflected on some of this commentary, I was reminded of the story of the blind beggar in John chapter 9. Recall that a question was raised of this poor man and his blindness: *Who sinned*—him or his parents—to cause his blindness? [see verse 2]. After Jesus miraculously heals him, the Pharisees wanted to investigate what happened. They call for the beggar, interrogate him, and they ask for his own testimony about who Jesus is and whether *he* is a sinner. And recall his famous "Whether or not he is a sinner I do not know. . . . But here is what I do know—I was blind and now I can see" [see verse 25].

So when people ask, "What will happen next? What will be the long-term ramifications?" Or whether or not this was a revival . . . I do not know. But like that blind beggar, I can say, "Here is what I do know." I know that fifty thousand hungry-hearted people came to a space to seek Jesus. I saw raw confession, radical humility, and life-altering commitments being made. I know there was a movement among us. I know it was sweet, gentle, beautiful, good, right, and true. I know people were freed from crippling strongholds in their lives. I know this was something more than collective effervescence or social contagion. I know that we will never be the same.

I also know this didn't start because of human effort or ingenuity. This did not take place because of our venue. It was not a function of preplanned leadership or a project committee. It could not be tracked to a professional worship band or celebrity speakers. It was not a product of expensive marketing or a professional advertising campaign. What I observed was a deep and trenchant hunger, a kind of desperation for something deeper, more genuine, more real, and more fulfilling.[66]

President Brown recalled blind Bartimaeus whom Jesus, for heaven's sake, did not pass by. Nor did he pass by many an Asbury student; nor did he pass by many a penitent who came to tiny Wilmore from across the nation and across the globe; nor did he pass by this author. Praise God from whom all blessings flow.

appendix b

CHRONOLOGY: FEBRUARY 8–24, 2023

Wednesday 2/8 High Temp: 57°	Rev. Zach Meerkreebs, Lexington First Alliance Church, speaks in chapel in Hughes Auditorium, 10:00–10:50 a.m. Several members of the gospel choir continue singing, and approximately 30 students remain to pray after chapel. Texts, word of mouth, and singing prompt other students to return. Some 200 to 250 students are worshipping in Hughes by the afternoon, 300 to 400 by evening. The Asbury *Collegian* posts its first media account of revival. Students arrive from the University of Kentucky, Eastern Kentucky University, Western Kentucky University, Ohio Christian University, and Indiana Wesleyan University. TikTok views: 10 million
Wednesday 2/8– Thursday 2/9 High Temp: 57° High Temp: 73°	Hundreds of students are worshipping in Hughes at 11:00 p.m., with approximately 25 to 30 students remaining through the night. Worship includes singing, reciting of Scripture, some praying in small groups, others kneeling at the altar, some sharing with one another.

Thursday 2/9 High Temp: 73°	Hundreds of students are worshipping by midmorning. By afternoon students are arriving from other parts of Kentucky and also from Tennessee, Ohio, Indiana, and Michigan. By evening Hughes is standing room only, including additional students from the University of the Cumberlands, Georgetown College, Transylvania University, Midway University, Purdue University, Lee University, and Mt. Vernon Nazarene University.
Friday 2/10 High Temp: 48°	Hughes is near capacity (1,500), with visitors now in the majority. Lines begin to form to enter Hughes.
Saturday 2/11 High Temp: 50°	Hughes is over capacity. Well over half in attendance are visitors. Communion is served to approximately 1,500 worshippers.
Sunday 2/12 High Temp: 57°	Students from at least 22 colleges and universities arrive on campus. Asbury Seminary opens overflow venues in Estes Chapel, McKenna Chapel, and the Cowen Building (the former Free Methodist sanctuary), the latter for one day only. From 50 students worshipping in Hughes at 3:00 a.m., numbers swell during the day to an estimated 3,000 (mostly visitors) worshipping in all venues. The Super Bowl has no effect on full-capacity worship.
Monday 2/13 High Temp: 63°	*Christianity Today* publishes its first article on the revival. CBN airs the first of at least nine reports on the revival. Unplanned, extended worship begins at Lee University (TN) and Campbellsville University (KY). Hughes, Estes, and McKenna are again full to capacity.

Tuesday 2/14
High Temp: 64°

Asbury University President Kevin Brown issues an open letter expressing gratitude for "such an inspiring expression of God's presence on our campus" but realizes "the influx of visitors" is causing "a degree of unsettledness among our students." He pledges to both "faithfully steward their university experience as well as this generous outpouring of God's Spirit on our campus." Asbury Seminary President Timothy Tennent posts "Thoughts on the Asbury Awakening": "What we are doggedly seeking is not lasting memories, but transformed lives." Unplanned, extended worship begins at Cedarville University (OH). The Great Commission Fellowship/ Wilmore United Methodist Church sanctuary opens as an overflow venue with simulcast. *Decision Magazine* covers the revival, followed by a cover story in the April 2023 issue.

Wednesday 2/15
High Temp: 73°

Attendance in Asbury Seminary 11:00 a.m. chapel service is over capacity. The *Washington Post* and NBC News run articles on the revival. Tucker Carlson, Fox News, interviews Asbury University student body president Alison Perfater on air. Extended unscheduled worship begins at Samford University (AL). Unscheduled worship and baptisms take place at Northern Kentucky University. TikTok views: 24.4 million

Thursday 2/16
High Temp: 62°
heavy rain

"After much prayer and discussion with campus leadership," President Kevin Brown announces worship schedule changes in an effort to balance public opportunities for worship with "a more sustainable campus experience for our students." Afternoon and evening services are to continue through 2/19, with priority seating for youth ages 16 to 25. Lines hold fast despite heavy, cold rain at night.
TikTok views: 34.5 million

Friday 2/17
High Temp: 46°

Hughes closes at 1:00 a.m. for cleaning and staff and volunteer recuperation, but worship team music continues through the night. Hughes reopens for the public following the 10:00 a.m. chapel. Gen Z students continue to be offered seating preference. At 5:00 p.m. Mt. Freedom Baptist Church opens as an additional overflow venue in response to very large numbers of visitors waiting in line to enter Hughes. Kentucky State Police divert traffic from overloaded Route 39 to the less-congested Route 1268 into Wilmore. Tucker Carlson, Fox News, thanks Asbury for not inviting him to campus.

Saturday 2/18
High Temp: 46°

Wilmore more than doubles in size as the town is inundated by an estimated 7,000–15,000 out-of-town visitors. The university erects two outdoor screens facing the campus semicircle for simulcasts of Hughes worship. University and public officials share concern over the large number of visitors stretching the capacity of the Asbury institutions and the community. An estimated 20,000 visitors travel to Wilmore over the weekend. CNN runs a story on the revival, and the *Washington Post* publishes a second article. Asbury Seminary opens its gymnasium and cafeteria as overflow venues.
TikTok views: 63 million

Sunday 2/19– Monday 2/20 High Temp: 61°– High Temp: 57°	The university hosts the last days of services open to the general public as Wilmore traffic congestion exceeds capacity. To accommodate interest in the revival, the university begins live streaming of evening worship in Hughes on February 19, to continue through February 23. TikTok views: 68 million
Tuesday 2/21– Wednesday 2/22 High Temp: 60°– High Temp: 73°	Evening services in Hughes are held for high school and college youth, ages 16–25, with limited adult participation. Most participants are visitors to Wilmore.
Thursday 2/23 High Temp: 73° rain	Asbury hosts a previously scheduled Collegiate Day of Prayer in Hughes. The auditorium is near capacity. The event includes a simulcast to over 4,000 colleges and universities, 59 countries, and 9 million Facebook users.
Friday 2/24 High Temp: 48°	*The New York Times* and *The Atlantic* publish articles on the Asbury Revival. The "Jesus Revolution" film premiers nationwide featuring the 1970's youth movement of spiritual renewal.

appendix c

WORSHIP MUSIC

Crossover *	Tags**	Hymns	CCM***	Gospel	Linguistic****
Be Glorified	Amazing Grace	O How I Love Jesus	Kings of Kings	You Deserve It	Baba
Friend of God	Christ the Solid Rock I Stand	How Great Thou Art	Christ Be Magnified	You Are the Living Word	To the One Seated on the Throne
Promises	Sanctuary	Holy, Holy, Holy	Living Hope	Awesome	Our Father
Jesus at the Center	At the Cross	It Is Well	O Praise the Name	I Give Myself Away	Jesus, Jesus, Jesus
You Are Alpha and Omega	I Thank God	Jesus Paid It All	Holy Ground	With Hiding Nothing	God You're So Good
Agnus Dei	This Altar	Great Is Thy Faithfulness	Reign About It All	Mighty One	Good Good Father
Spirit Break Out	If God	Blessed Assurance	Build My Life	More Than Anything	Imela
Firm Foundation	We Lift on High	Come Thou Fount	Worthy of It All	Every Praise	
New Wine	I Exalt You	The Blood (Will Never Lose Its Power)	Hymn of Heaven	The Anthem	
Here I Am to Worship	Wide as the Sky	In Christ Alone	From the Inside Out	Revelation 19	
Way Maker	Be Praised	Pass Me Not	Gratitude	For Your Glory	
Goodness of God	Give Us Clean Hands	Because He Lives	Closer	He Is Able	
Resurrecting	To the One Who Is Seated on the Throne	Tis So Sweet	Gracias	I Won't Go Back	
Most Beautiful	The Cross Has the Final Word		Forever	Made a Way	
You Are Good	Ever Be		Jesus You're Beautiful	My Life Is in Your Hands	

* Crossover: blend of Gospel and Contemporary Christian Music
**Tag: a refrain rather than a full song
***Christian Contemporary Music (CCM)
****Linguistic: easy to sing in multiple languages

Crossover*	Tags**	Hymns	CCM***	Gospel	Linguistic****
The Blessing	Gracefully Broken		All Hail King Jesus	No Body Greater	
Rest on Us	Everlasting Arms		He Is Exalted	Run Over	
House of Miracles	Let the Redeemed		Run to the Father	The Call	
Yes and Amen	Fight My Battles		Oh Come to the Altar	Completely Yes	
Nothing Else	I Love You Forever		Lead Me to the Cross	No Bondage	
I Speak Jesus			Hosanna	Make Room	
Defender			Set a Fire	Let Praise Rise	
See a Victory			Champion	Moving Forward	
Break Every Chain			Yes I Will	Nothing Without You	
Fill Me Up			Is He Worthy	Lord You Are Good	
Heart of Worship			You Give Joy		
Open the Eyes			Indescribable		
How Great Is Our God			Your Love Never Fails		
Our God			God I Look to You		
Have My Heart			Here as in Heaven		
King of Glory			Too Good to Not Believe		
Be Praised			House of Miracles		

* Crossover: blend of Gospel and Contemporary Christian Music
** Tag: a refrain rather than a full song
*** Christian Contemporary Music (CCM)
**** Linguistic: easy to sing in multiple languages

Asbury University Chaplain Greg Haseloff, Chapel Coordinator Madeline Black, and several students identified the following list of twenty songs most frequently sung during the outpouring.

Agnus Dei
Break Every Chain
Closer
Glorious Day
Goodness of God
Gratitude
Great Are You Lord
Here I Am to Worship
Holy, Holy, Holy
I Exalt Thee
Jesus, We Love You
King of Kings
Make Room
Mighty One
Reign Above It All
Resurrecting
Run to the Father
Waymaker
Withholding Nothing / I Give Myself Away
Worthy of It All

appendix d

COLLEGES AND UNIVERSITIES REPRESENTED AT THE ASBURY OUTPOURING

*Most institutions were identified by Diane Troyer from a whiteboard in the lobby of Hughes Auditorium. In some cases, handwritten abbreviations could apply to more than one school, hence entries with two potential institutions and locations.

Abraham Baldwin Agricultural College	GA
Allen College	IA
Anderson University	IN
Angelo State University	TX
Appalachian State University	NC
Arkansas State University	AR
Asbury Theological Seminary	KY
Asbury University	KY
Assemblies of God Theological Seminary	MO
Athens Technical College	GA
Auburn University	AL
Baldwin Wallace University	OH

Ball State University	IN
Baylor University	TX
Belhaven University	MS
Belmont University	TN
Berea College	KY
Bethel School of Supernatural Ministry	CA
Bethel University (Mishawaka)	IN
Bethel University (St. Paul)	MN
Biola University	CA
Bluegrass Community and Technical College	KY
Bob Jones University	SC
Bowling Green State University	KY
Boyce College	KY
Bryan College	TN
Bunker Hill Community College	MA
Butler University	IN
California Lutheran University	CA
California State University Northridge	CA
Calvin University	MI
Campbellsville University	KY
Cedarville University	OH
Centre College	KY
Charis Bible College	CO
Charleston Southern University	SC
Chattanooga State Community College	TN
Claremont School of Theology	CA
Clemson University	SC
Cleveland Institute of Art or Culinary Institute of America	OH/NY*
Cleveland State University	OH
College of DuPage	IL
College of the Albemarle	SC
Colorado School of Mines	CO

Columbus State University	GA
Cornerstone University	MI
Cornerstone University	TN
Covenant College	GA
Cumberland University	TN
Davidson Davie Community College	NC
Denison University	OH
Des Moines Area Community College	IA
Duke University	NC
East Central College or	
Elgin Community College	MO/IL*
East Tennessee State University	TN
Eastern Illinois University	IL
Eastern Kentucky University	KY
Eastern Michigan University	MI
Elim Bible Institute and College	NY
Emmanuel Christian College	OH
Emmanuel College	GA
Emmaus Bible College	IA
Emory University	GA
Faculdade Independente do Nordeste	Brazil
Florida Atlantic University	FL
Florida International University	FL
Florida Southern College	FL
Freedom City Bible College	MO
Friends University	KS
Gardner-Webb University	GA
Gateway Community & Technical College	KY
George Mason University	VA
Georgetown College	KY
Georgia State University	GA
Georgia Tech University	GA
God's Bible School	OH

Gordon College	MA
Gordon-Conwell Theological Seminary	MA
Grand Canyon University	AZ
Grand Valley State University	MI
Greenville Technical College	SC
Guilford Technical Community College	NC
Hannibal-LaGrange University	MO
Hardin-Simmons University	TX
Harding University	AR
Hillsdale College	MI
Hillsong College	Australia
Hofstra University	TX
Houston Community College	TX
Hudson Valley Community College	NY
Huntington College	IN
Illinois State University or	
Iowa State University	IL/IA*
International House of Prayer University	MO
Indiana Purdue Fort Wayne	IN
Indiana State University	IN
Indiana University	IN
Indiana University Southeast	IN
Indiana University-Purdue University Indianapolis	IN
Indiana Wesleyan University	IN
Ivy Tech Community College	MO
John Brown University	AR
John Jay College of Criminal Justice	NY
Judson University	IL
Kalamazoo College	MI
Kanakuk Institute	MO
Kankakee Community College	IL
Kansas State University	KS
Kean University	NJ

Kent State University	OH
Kentucky Christian University	KY
Kentucky Mountain Bible College	KY
Kentucky State University	KY
Kettering University	MI
Lead College	LA
Lee University	TN
LeTourneau University	TX
Liberty University	TN
Lindsey Wilson College	KY
Lipscomb University	TN
Louisiana State University	LA
Madisonville Community College or Marshalltown Community College	KY/IA*
Malone University	OH
Manchester University	IN
Marshall University	WV
Miami University	OH
Michigan State University	MI
Middle Tennessee State University	TN
Midway University	KY
Midwestern University	IL
Milligan University	TN
Milwaukee School of Engineering	WI
Minnesota State University	MN
Mississippi State University	MS
Mississippi University for Women	MS
Missouri Baptist University	MO
Monmouth College	IL
Montana State University	MT
Monteverde Academy	FL
Montreal College	Canada
Moody Bible Institute	IL

Moody Theological Seminary	IL
Morehead State University	KY
Mount Vernon Nazarene University	OH
Murray State University	KY
Myrtle Beach College	SC
Nashotah House Theological Seminary	WI
Nazarene Theological Seminary	KS
New York University	NY
North Carolina State University	NC
Northeast Missouri State University	MO
Northeastern University	MA
Northern Illinois University	IL
Northern Kentucky University	KY
Northpoint Bible College	MI
Northrop University	MN
Nuclear Power School	SC
Oakland University	MI
Odessa University	TX
Ohio Christian University	OH
Ohio State University	OH
Ohio Technical College	OH
Ohio Wesleyan University	OH
Okanagan College	Canada
Olivet Nazarene University	IL
Online Bible College	Thailand
Oral Roberts University	OK
Ouachita Baptist University	AR
Palm Beach Atlantic University	FL
Pennsylvania State University	PA
Pikes Peak Community College	CO
Point Loma Nazarene University	CA
Purdue University	IN
Quincy University	IL

Randolph-Macon College	VA
Regent College	Canada
Regent University	VA
Rhema Bible Training College	OK
Rio de Janeiro University	Brazil
Rockhurst University	MO
Rogers State University	OK
Rutgers University	NJ
Samford McWhorter University	AL
Samford University	AL
Savannah College of Art & Design	GA
Shawnee State University	OH
South Dakota State University	SD
Southeast Kentucky Community & Tech College	KY
Southeast Missouri State	MO
Southeastern Louisiana University	LA
Southern Baptist Theological Seminary	KY
Southern Evangelical Seminary	NC
Southern Illinois University	IL
Southern New Hampshire University	NH
Southern Regional Technical College	GA
Southern Wesleyan University	SC
Southwestern Assemblies of God University	TX
Spring Arbor University	MI
St. Louis Community College	MO
State University of Maranhão	Brazil
Sul Ross State University	TX
Syracuse University	NY
Tallahassee Community College or Tidewater Community College	FL/VA*
Tarleton State University	TX
Taylor University	IN
Tennessee Tech	TN

Texas A & M	TX
The College of Saint Rose	NY
The Ramp School of Ministry	AL
Three Rivers College	MO
Toledo Symphony School of Music	OH
Transylvania University	KY
Trevecca Nazarene University	TN
Trinity Christian College	IL
Trinity International University	IL
Tyndale University	Canada
United Theological Seminary	OH
Universidade da Região de Joinville	Brazil
Universidade de Campina	Brazil
University of Akron	OH
University of Alabama in Huntsville	AL
University of Alaska	AK
University of Albany	NY
University of Arkansas	AR
University of Cincinnati	OH
University of Evansville	IN
University of Georgia	GA
University of Houston of North Texas	TX
University of Illinois	IL
University of Indianapolis	IN
University of Kentucky	KY
University of Louisville	KY
University of Mary Hardin-Baylor	TX
University of Maryland	MD
University of Memphis	TN
University of Miami	FL
University of Mobile	AL
University of Nebraska/Lincoln	NE
University of New Mexico	NM

University of North Dakota	ND
University of North Georgia	GA
University of Notre Dame	IN
University of Pittsburgh	PA
University of Richmond or	
University of Rochester	VA/NY*
University of Southern Indiana	IN
University of St. Francis	IL
University of Tennessee	TN
University of Texas at Dallas	TX
University of Texas at San Antonio	TX
University of the Cumberlands	KY
University of Valley Forge	PA
University of Virginia	VA
University of Virginia at Wise	VA
University of West Florida	FL
University of Wisconsin	WI
University of Wisconsin-La Crosse	WI
Valencia College	FL
Valor Christian College	OH
Vanguard University	CA
Victory College	OK
Viña del Mar University	Chile
Vincennes University	IN
Virginia Tech University	VA
Volunteer State Community College	TN
Washburn University	KS
Washtenaw Community College (WCC)	MI
Welch College	TN
West Virginia University	WV
Western Kentucky University	KY
Western Michigan University	MI
Wheaton College	IL

Winthrop University	SC
Wiregrass Georgia Technical College, Ben Hill Campus	GA
Word of Life Bible Institute	NY
Wright State University	OH
Xavier University	OH
Yale Divinity School	CT
Youngstown State University	OH
Youth with a Mission, Kona	HI
Youth with a Mission	New Zealand

notes

FOREWORD

1. Richard Owen Roberts, *Revival* (Carol Stream, IL: Tyndale House Publishers, 1982), 107.

PREFACE

1. Fanny Crosby, "Pass Me Not," 1868. Public domain.
2. Russell T. McCutcheon, ed., *The Insider/Outsider Problem in the Study of Religion* (London: Cassell Academic, 1999).

INTRODUCTION

1. Kevin Brown, "An Update from Asbury University," February 14, 2023. For a fine, brief survey of nineteenth- and twentieth-century US college and university revivals, see Michael F. Gleason, *When God Walked on Campus: A Brief History of Evangelical Awakenings at American Colleges and Universities* (Dundas, Ontario: Joshua Press, 2002). An older study by the most prolific student of revival history is J. Edwin Orr, *Campus Aflame: Evangelical Awakenings in Collegiate Communities* (Glendale, CA: G/L Publications, 1971).
2. Edward McKinley and Jonathan Kulaga, eds., *A Purpose Rare: 125 Years of Asbury University* (Wilmore, KY: Asbury University, 2015), 22–24; Phillip B. Collier, "The Significance of the Asbury Revival of 1970 for Some Aspects of the Spiritual

Lives of the Participants," D. Min. thesis, Asbury Theological Seminary, 1995.

3. Jean M. Twenge, "Increases in Depression, Self-Harm, and Suicide among U.S. Adolescents after 2012 and Links to Technology Use: Possible Mechanisms," *Psychiatry Online*, March 27, 2020.

4. Robert Kanary, "The Long but Little-Known History," *Salvo Magazine* blog, February 27, 2023; Lawson Stone, Revival Diary, based on Facebook posts, February 8–24, 2023; emailed to author, April 3, 2023.

5. Keith Hardman, *Seasons of Refreshing: Evangelism and Revivals in America* (Grand Rapids, MI: Baker Books, 1994), 16.

6. J. Edwin Orr, *Times of Refreshing* (London: Marshall, Morgan, & Scott, 1936), 127, emphasis mine.

7. Orr, *Times*, 127.

8. Henry C. James et al., *Halls Aflame: An Account of the Spontaneous Revivals at Asbury College in 1950 and 1958* (Wilmore, KY: First Fruits Press, 2013), 44, emphasis mine.

9. Suzanne Nicholson, "When Streams of Living Water Become a Flood: Revival at Asbury University," *Firebrand Magazine*, February 21, 2023, emphasis mine, https://firebrandmag.com/articles/when-streams-of-living-water-become-a-flood-revival-at-asbury-university.

CHAPTER ONE: SPIRITUAL SPONTANEOUS COMBUSTION

1. Greg Haseloff email, May 12, 2023.

2. Kevin Brown, livestream to Avon Park Camp Meeting, Avon Park, Florida, February 10, 2023.

3. David Thomas interview, April 19, 2023; CBN, "The Asbury Awakening."

4. Rev. Zach Meerkreebs chapel, Love in Action Series, February 8, 2023; www.asbury.edu.

5. Meerkreebs, "Love in Action" Series, February 8, 2023.

6. Reports on the number of additional worshippers who stayed to pray after 10:50 frequently mention 19 to 20. Sharing in a retired faculty prayer meeting, April 11, 2023, freshman Mary

Hosteller was among those who prayed in Hughes after chapel, and remembers about 30 who remained. Chaplain Haseloff, who double-checked chapel video footage, believes the figure is "closer to 35," mostly students, but including about six staff. His assistant, Madeline Black, on the scene, estimates 30 to 40 stayed after chapel. Greg Haseloff interview, April 5, 2023; Madeline Black interview, April 21, 2023.

7. Lena Marlowe, YouTube video interview with Cameron Bertuzi, "Capturing Christianity," February 27, 2023.

8. Deborah Laker, "Two Asbury Students Reflect on What the Revival Means for Gen Z's Faith," *Religion Unplugged*, February 22, 2023, https://religionunplugged.com/news/2023/2/22/what -the-asbury-revival-means-for-gen-zs-faith.

9. Madeline Coggins, "'Incredible' Stories of Healing, Reconciliation Emerge from Christian Revival at Kentucky College," *Fox News*, February 22, 2023, https://www.foxnews .com/media/incredible-stories-healing-reconciliation-emerge -christian-revival-kentucky-college.

10. Madeline Black interview, April 21, 2023.

11. Steve Seamands, Thoughtful Fellowship Book Club, April 5, 2023; Rob Lim interview, May 2, 2023.

12. Daniel Silliman, "'No Celebrities Except Jesus': How Asbury Protected the Revival," *Christianity Today*, February 23, 2023, https://www.christianitytoday.com/news/2023/february /asbury-revival-outpouring-protect-work-admin-volunteers .html.

13. Kevin Brown, livestream, Avon Park, February 10, 2023; CBN, "The Asbury Awakening."

14. Kevin Brown email, May 11, 2023.

15. David Thomas interview, April 19, 2023.

16. Sarah Baldwin interview, March 24, 2023.

17. Gregg A. Okesson, "Asbury Provost Reflects on Revival," Association of Theological Schools, *Colloquy Online*, March 2023, https://www.ats.edu/files/galleries/asbury-provost-reflects -on-revival.pdf.

18. Timothy Tennent interview, March 29, 2023.

19. Jeffrey Rickman, "Interview with Jonathan Powers," *PlainSpoken*, YouTube, February 16, 2023.

20. Sherry Powers interview, April 24, 2023.

21. Steve Seamands, Thoughtful Fellowship Book Club, April 5, 2023.

22. Rob Lim interview, May 2, 2023.

23. Suzanne Nicholson, "When Streams of Living Water Become a Flood: Revival at Asbury University," *Firebrand Magazine*, February 21, 2023, https://firebrandmag.com/articles/when-streams-of-living-water-become-a-flood-revival-at-asbury-university.

24. David Thomas interview, April 19, 2023.

25. Sarah Baldwin interview, March 24, 2023; Madeline Black interview, April 21, 2023.

26. Sarah Baldwin interview, March 24, 2023.

27. Steve Rehner email to friends, February 20, 2023.

28. Nicholson, "When Streams of Living Water Become a Flood."

29. Jerry Coleman, "Notes from Jerry—February," February 22, 2023.

30. Brandon Porter, "Revival Fires Stir Again at Asbury," *Baptist Press*, February 12, 2023, https://www.baptistpress.com/resource-library/news/revival-fires-stir-again-at-asbury/.

31. Bill Elliff, "Reflections from Asbury (Part 1)," blog, February 11, 2023, https://billelliff.org/blogs/news/reflections-from-asbury.

32. Tim Beougher, Facebook post, February 13, 2023.

33. Gregg A. Okesson, "Asbury Provost Reflects on Revival."

34. Tom McCall, "Asbury Professor: We're Witnessing a 'Surprising Work of God,'" *Christianity Today*, February 13, 2023, https://www.christianitytoday.com/ct/2023/february-web-only/asbury-revival-1970-2023-methodist-christian-holy-spirit.html.

35. Gina Christian, "'Jesus Was Right Next to Me': Asbury Revival Sets Catholics on Fire with Holy Spirit," *Detroit Catholic*, February 17, 2023, https://www.detroitcatholic.com/news/jesus-was-right-next-to-me-asbury-revival-sets-catholics-on-fire-with-holy-spirit.

36. Larry Brown interview, April 28, 2023.

37. Lawson Stone, Revival Diary, February 8–24, 2023.

38. Timothy Tennent, "Thoughts on the Asbury Awakening," blog, February 14, 2023, https://timothytennent.com/thoughts -on-the-asbury-awakening/.

CHAPTER TWO: THE BACKSTORY

1. Henry C. James et al., *Halls Aflame: An Account of the Spontaneous Revivals at Asbury College in 1950 and 1958* (Wilmore, KY: First Fruits Press, 2013); Robert Kanary, *Spontaneous Revivals: Asbury College 1905–2006: Firsthand Accounts of Lives Transformed* (Lexington, KY: CreateSpace, 2017). The fullest accounts of the 1970 revival are Robert E. Coleman, ed., *One Divine Moment: The Account of the Asbury Revival of 1970*, Anniversary Edition (1970; repr., Wilmore, KY: First Fruits Press, 2013); and Wayne Atcheson, *The Asbury Revival: When God Used Students to Wake a Nation* (Hartselle, AL: Soncoast Publishing, 2020). See also Joseph Thacker, *Asbury College: Vision and Miracle* (Nappanee, IN: Evangel Press, 1990); and Edward McKinley and Jonathan Kulaga, eds., *A Purpose Rare: 125 Years of Asbury University* (Wilmore, KY: Asbury University, 2015).

2. Thacker, *Asbury College* (51–52), and McKinley, *A Purpose Rare* (123), give 1905 for the date of the revival, while Kanary, *Spontaneous Revivals* (18), dates it to 1907.

3. Kanary, *Spontaneous Revivals*, 77–79.

4. James, *Halls Aflame*, i.

5. Atcheson, *The Asbury Revival*.

6. Paul Prather, "History Repeats Itself as Another Spontaneous Revival Sweeps Asbury University," *Lexington Herald-Leader*, February 16, 2023, https://www.aol.com/news/history-repeats -itself-another-spontaneous-163446099.html.

7. Phillip B. Collier, "The Significance of the Asbury Revival of 1970 for Some Aspects of the Spiritual Lives of the Participants," D. Min. thesis, Asbury Theological Seminary, 1995, 46. The Asbury University website notes 144 consecutive hours for the 1970 revival.

8. Lawson Stone, Revival Diary, February 8–24, 2023.

9. McKinley, *A Purpose Rare*, 124.

10. Daniel Silliman, "'No Celebrities Except Jesus': How Asbury Protected the Revival," *Christianity Today*, February 23, 2023, https://www.christianitytoday.com/news/2023/february/asbury -revival-outpouring-protect-work-admin-volunteers.html.

11. W. R. Ward, *The Protestant Evangelical Awakening* (Cambridge: Cambridge University Press, 1992); J. Edwin Orr, *The Flaming Tongue: The Impact of Twentieth Century Revivals* (Chicago: Moody Press, 1973).

12. J. Edwin Orr's volumes on the history of revival are too numerous to note here. For a biographical sketch of Orr and an introduction to his writings on revival, see Michael A. G. Haykin, "J. Edwin Orr, 1912–1982: Historian of Revival," in Michael F. Gleason, *When God Walked on Campus*, 131–35.

13. Haadiza Ogwude, "A Nonstop Revival Breaks Out at Kentucky College. Now It's Viral on TikTok," *Louisville Courier-Journal*, February 20, 2023, https://www.cincinnati.com /story/news/2023/02/16/what-is-a-revival-asbury-university -revival-service-going-viral-tiktok/69910880007/; Ward, *The Protestant Evangelical Awakening*.

14. Dr. Victor Hamilton, retired Asbury University professor of Old Testament, in addition to confirming the nineteen references to being filled with the Holy Spirit, notes many additional passages describe the Spirit's coming upon especially Old Testament figures, including elders, judges, and David. Victor Hamilton email, May 11, 2023.

15. A vast literature exists on the theology and history of revival and its synonym approximations: awakening, outpouring, renewal, and revitalization. A helpful introduction to the concept with judicious annotated notes is Robert E. Coleman, "What Is Revival?" in *Accounts of a Campus Revival: Wheaton College 1995*, edited by Timothy K. Beougher and Lyle W. Dorsett (Wheaton, IL: Harold Shaw Publishers, 1995), 13–29. The dean of the history of revival movements is J. Edwin Orr, author of a score of books on the subject, some with a

chronological and some with a geographic focus. A helpful summary treatment is his 64-page booklet, *The Re-Study of Revival and Revivalism* (Pasadena, CA: School of World Mission, 1981).

16. Jean M. Twenge, "Increases in Depression, Self-Harm, and Suicide among U.S. Adolescents after 2012 and Links to Technology Use: Possible Mechanisms," *Psychiatry Online*, March 27, 2020; Ryan P. Burge, "Gen Z and Religion in 2021," *Religion in Public*, June 15, 2022, https://religioninpublic.blog/2022/06/15/gen-z-and-religion-in-2021/; Liza Evseeva and Jake Traylor, "A Nonstop Kentucky Prayer 'Revival' Is Going Viral on TikTok, and People Are Traveling Thousands of Miles to Take Part," NBC News, February 15, 2023, https://www.nbcnews.com/tech/internet/asbury-university-revival-college-kentucky-going-viral-tiktok-rcna70686; James Emery White, *Meet Generation Z: Understanding and Reaching the New Post-Christian World* (Grand Rapids, MI: Baker Books, 2017), 49; [Jon Williams], "A Christian College in Kentucky Has Experienced a Religious Awakening," *The Economist*, February 23, 2023, 8.

17. Terry Mattingly, "At Asbury, 2023 Revival Has Been 'Déjà vu All Over Again,'" *Hastings Tribune*, February 24, 2023, https://www.hastingstribune.com/on-religion-at-asbury-2023-revival-has-been-deja-vu-all-over-again/article_4d2b10be-b4a1-11ed-be68-c34a354420e6.html.

18. Twenge, "Increases in Depression."

19. Ruth Graham, "'Woodstock,' for Christians: Revival Draws Thousands to Kentucky Town," *New York Times*, February 20, 2023, https://www.nytimes.com/2023/02/23/us/kentucky-revival-asbury-university.html.

20. Aaron Griffith, "What Asbury's Christian Revival Says about America's Need for Connection," *Time Magazine*, February 28, 2023, https://time.com/6258703/asbury-christian-revival-america-connection/.

21. Prather, "History Repeats Itself."

22. Gina Christian, "'Jesus Was Right Next to Me': Asbury Revival Sets Catholics on Fire with Holy Spirit," *Detroit Catholic*,

February 17, 2023, https://www.detroitcatholic.com/news/jesus-was-right-next-to-me-asbury-revival-sets-catholics-on-fire-with-holy-spirit.

23. Alexandra Presta, "Learning to Love: A Sunday Night Revival Update," *Asbury Collegian*, February 12, 2023, http://www.theasburycollegian.com/2023/02/learning-to-love-a-sunday-night-revival-update/.

24. Jon Brown, "Christian University in Kentucky Draws Pilgrims Nationwide Amid Spiritual Revival: 'Gives Me So Much Hope,'" Fox News, February, 2023, https://www.foxnews.com/us/christian-university-kentucky-draws-pilgrims-nationwide-spiritual-revival-gives-me-so-much-hope.

25. Sarah Baldwin, Facebook post, February 16, 2023.

26. Thacker, *Asbury College*, 222; Collier, "The Significance of the Asbury Revival of 1970 for Some Aspects of the Spiritual Lives of the Participants," 36.

27. Mary Hosteller, retired faculty prayer meeting, April 11, 2023.

28. Tom McCall, "Asbury Professor: We're Witnessing a 'Surprising Work of God,'" *Christianity Today*, February 13, 2023, https://www.christianitytoday.com/ct/2023/february-web-only/asbury-revival-1970-2023-methodist-christian-holy-spirit.html.

29. Rob Lim interview, May 2, 2023; Steve Seamands, Thoughtful Fellowship Book Club, April 5, 2023; Silliman, "'No Celebrities.'"

30. Craig Keener, "Opinion: What Is Revival—and Is It Happening at Asbury?" February 16, 2023, https://julieroys.com/opinion-what-revival-happening-asbury/.

CHAPTER THREE: THE HEART OF WORSHIP

1. Laura Levens, "What I Witnessed This Week at the Asbury Revival," *Baptist News Global*, February 16, 2023, https://baptistnews.com/article/what-i-witnessed-this-week-at-the-asbury-revival/.

2. Suzanne Nicholson, "When Streams of Living Water Become a Flood: Revival at Asbury University," *Firebrand Magazine*, February 21, 2023, https://firebrandmag.com/articles/when

-streams-of-living-water-become-a-flood-revival-at-asbury
-university.

3. Deborah Laker, "Two Asbury Students Reflect on What the Revival Means for Gen Z's Faith," *Religion Unplugged*, February 22, 2023, https://religionunplugged.com/news/2023/2/22/what-the-asbury-revival-means-for-gen-zs-faith.

4. Sarah Baldwin interview, March 24, 2023.

5. Greg Haseloff, Wilmore Missions Network meeting, April 12, 2023.

6. J. D. Walt email, May 11, 2023.

7. Steve Seamands, Thoughtful Fellowship Book Club, April 5, 2023.

8. Daniel Silliman, "'No Celebrities Except Jesus': How Asbury Protected the Revival," *Christianity Today*, February 23, 2023, https://www.christianitytoday.com/news/2023/february/asbury-revival-outpouring-protect-work-admin-volunteers.html.

9. Liza Evseeva and Jake Traylor, "A Nonstop Kentucky Prayer 'Revival' Is Going Viral on TikTok, and People Are Traveling Thousands of Miles to Take Part," NBC News, February 15, 2023, https://www.nbcnews.com/tech/internet/asbury-university-revival-college-kentucky-going-viral-tiktok-rcna70686.

10. Paul Prather, "History Repeats Itself as Another Spontaneous Revival Sweeps Asbury University," *Lexington Herald-Leader*, February 16, 2023, https://www.aol.com/news/history-repeats-itself-another-spontaneous-163446099.html.

11. Steve Rehner email to friends, February 20, 2023.

12. Amber Ferguson, "Nonstop Worship Service at Kentucky College Set to End after Attracting Thousands," *Washington Post*, February 18, 2023, https://www.washingtonpost.com/religion/2023/02/18/asbury-university-revival-kentucky/.

13. Lawson Stone, Revival Diary, February 8–24, 2023.

14. Levens, "What I Witnessed This Week at the Asbury Revival"; J. D. Walt, interview with Andy King and Chuck Tate, Revival Town Podcast, February 23, 2023, revivaltownpodcast.com.

15. Bill Elliff, "First Person: Revival Reflections from Asbury (Part 3)," *The Baptist Paper*, February 14, 2023, https://the baptistpaper.org/first-person-revival-reflections-from-asbury/.

16. J. D. Walt, "Asbury Revival," Revival Town Podcast, February 26, 2023.

17. Mark Swayze interview, April 18, 2023.

18. Gina Christian, "'Jesus Was Right Next to Me': Asbury Revival Sets Catholics on Fire with Holy Spirit," *Detroit Catholic*, February 17, 2023, https://www.detroitcatholic.com/news /jesus-was-right-next-to-me-asbury-revival-sets-catholics-on -fire-with-holy-spirit.

19. Thomas Lyons, "Asbury Revival: Answers to Help Us Understand What God Might Be Up To," Seminary Now blogpost, February 14, 2023, https://seminarynow.com/pages /blog?p=asbury-revival-answers-to-help-us-understand.

20. Gregg A. Okesson, "Asbury Provost Reflects on Revival," Association of Theological Schools, *Colloquy Online*, March 2023, https://www.ats.edu/files/galleries/asbury-provost-reflects -on-revival.pdf.

21. Silliman, "'No Celebrities Except Jesus.'"

22. Sarah Baldwin, Facebook post, February 16, 2023.

23. Mark Whitworth interview, March 29, 2023.

24. Silliman, "'No Celebrities Except Jesus.'"

25. Thomas Lyons, "When a Christian Revival Goes Viral," *The Atlantic*, February 23, 2023, https://www.theatlantic.com /ideas/archive/2023/02/asbury-kentucky-university-christian -revival/673176/.

26. Suzanne Nicholson, "When Streams of Living Water Become a Flood"; Bill Elliff, "Reflections on Asbury (Part 5)," February 16, 2023, https://billelliff.org/blogs/news/reflections-on-asbury -part-5; Bill Elliff, "Reflections on Spiritual Awakening (Part 8)," February 24, 2023.

27. Evseeva and Traylor, "A Nonstop Kentucky Prayer 'Revival' Is Going Viral on TikTok."

28. Lyons, "When a Christian Revival Goes Viral."

29. Levens, "What I Witnessed This Week at the Asbury Revival."

30. Lyons, "When a Christian Revival Goes Viral."

31. Rehner email to friends, February 20, 2023.

32. Christian, "'Jesus Was Right Next to Me.'"

33. "Statement from Dr. Kevin J. Brown on Thursday, February 14, 2023," Asbury University website; Kevin Brown, "Outpouring Video Description," attachment to email, May 11, 2023.

34. Timothy Tennent, "Thoughts on the Asbury Awakening," February 14, 2023, https://timothytennent.com/thoughts-on -the-asbury-awakening/.

35. Tom McCall, "Asbury Professor: We're Witnessing a 'Surprising Work of God,'" *Christianity Today*, February 13, 2023, https:// www.christianitytoday.com/ct/2023/february-web-only/asbury -revival-1970-2023-methodist-christian-holy-spirit.html.

36. Yale Kim, "Eyewitness Report: A Spiritual Revival Is Breaking Out at Asbury University in Kentucky—Could It Spread Across the Country and World?" February 16, 2023, https://allisrael .com/eyewitness-report-a-spiritual-revival-is-breaking-out-at -asbury-university-in-kentucky-could-it-spread-across-the -country-and-world.

37. Stevan Sheets, Facebook post, February 14, 2023.

38. David Thomas interview, April 19, 2023.

39. Keith Madill interview, February 21, 2023.

40. Lyons, "Asbury Revival."

41. McCall, "Asbury Professor."

42. Bill Elliff, "Reflections from Asbury (Part 3)," blog, February 14, 2023, https://billelliff.org/blogs/news/reflections-from -asbury-part-3?_pos=5&_sid=dfa3e5a2d&_ss=r.

43. Ben Witherington, "The Asbury Revival Rolls On," February 17, 2023, https://www.patheos.com/blogs/bibleandculture/2023/02 /17/the-asbury-revival-rolls-on/.

CHAPTER FOUR: TRANSFORMED IN WORSHIP

1. Jerry Coleman, "Notes from Jerry," February 22, 2023.

2. David Thomas interview, April 19, 2023.

3. Deborah Laker, "Two Asbury Students Reflect on What the Revival Means for Gen Z's Faith," *Religion Unplugged*, February

22, 2023, https://religionunplugged.com/news/2023/2/22/what-the-asbury-revival-means-for-gen-zs-faith.

4. Tim Beougher, Facebook post, February 13, 2023.

5. Alexandra Presta, "'He Is Enough'—The Asbury Revival Continues," *Asbury Collegian,* February 9, 2023, http://www.theasburycollegian.com/2023/02/learning-to-love-a-sunday-night-revival-update/.

6. Gina Christian, "'Jesus Was Right Next to Me': Asbury Revival Sets Catholics on Fire with Holy Spirit," *Detroit Catholic,* February 17, 2023, https://www.detroitcatholic.com/news/jesus-was-right-next-to-me-asbury-revival-sets-catholics-on-fire-with-holy-spirit.

7. Suzanne Nicholson, "When Streams of Living Water Become a Flood: Revival at Asbury University," *Firebrand Magazine,* February 21, 2023, https://firebrandmag.com/articles/when-streams-of-living-water-become-a-flood-revival-at-asbury-university.

8. Ruth Graham, "'Woodstock,' for Christians: Revival Draws Thousands to Kentucky Town," *New York Times,* February 20, 2023, https://www.nytimes.com/2023/02/23/us/kentucky-revival-asbury-university.html.

9. Christian, "'Jesus Was Right Next to Me.'"

10. Timothy Tennent interview, March 29, 2023; Greg Haseloff interview, April 5, 2023.

11. Robert Kanary, "The Long but Little-Known History," *Salvo Magazine* blog, February 27, 2023, https://salvomag.com/post/asbury-university-revivals.

12. Ben Witherington, "The Asbury Revival Rolls On," February 17, 2023, https://www.patheos.com/blogs/bibleandculture/2023/02/17/the-asbury-revival-rolls-on/; https://www.patheos.com.

13. Lawson Stone, Revival Diary, February 8–24, 2023.

14. Thomas Lyons, "When a Christian Revival Goes Viral," *The Atlantic,* February 23, 2023, https://www.theatlantic.com/ideas/archive/2023/02/asbury-kentucky-university-christian-revival/673176/.

15. Sarah Baldwin interview, March 24, 2023.

16. Nicholson, "When Streams of Living Water Become a Flood."
17. Sarah Baldwin interview, March 24, 2023.
18. Sarah Baldwin interview, March 24, 2023; Sarah Baldwin Facebook post, February 25, 2023.
19. Sarah Baldwin interview, March 24, 2023.
20. Larry Brown interview, April 28, 2023.
21. Rich Manieri, "Leave the Labels to History and Watch God Work," *Asbury Collegian*, February 24, 2023, https://www.theasburycollegian.com/2023/02/leave-the-labels-to-history-and-watch-god-work/.
22. Anna Lowe, "When the Dust Settles," *Asbury Collegian*, February 15, 2023, http://www.theasburycollegian.com/2023/02/when-the-dust-settles/.
23. Sara Clark, "Presence, Surrender, and Prayer: An Outpouring Testimony," *Asbury Collegian*, February 24, 2023, https://www.theasburycollegian.com/2023/02/presence-surrender-and-prayer-an-outpouring-testimony/.
24. Carolina Trumpower, "Persistent Peace: Attitudes and Habits after the Outpouring," *Asbury Collegian*, February 24, 2023, http://www.theasburycollegian.com/2023/02/persistent-peace-attitudes-and-habits-after-the-revival/.
25. "K. Q.," anonymous interview, April 5, 2023.
26. Bill Elliff, "Reflections on Asbury (Part 2)," February 13, 2023, https://billelliff.org/blogs/news/reflections-from-asbury-part-2?_pos=6&_sid=7958bf228&_ss=r.
27. Tim Beougher, Facebook post, February 13, 2023.

CHAPTER FIVE: LEADERSHIP AND LOGISTICS

1. Craig Keener, "Opinion: What Is Revival—and Is It Happening at Asbury?" February 16, 2023, https://julieroys.com/opinion-what-revival-happening-asbury/.
2. Kevin Brown, livestream, Avon Park, February 10, 2023; CBN, "The Asbury Awakening."
3. Jeannette Davis, retired faculty prayer meeting, March 14, 2023.
4. Paul Dupree interview, February 21, 2023; Mark Whitworth interview, March 29, 2023; Sarah Baldwin interview, March

24, 2023; Andy Miller interview, February 21, 2023; Kevin Brown email, May 11, 2023.

5. Sherry Powers interview, April 24, 2023.

6. Kevin Brown, "An Update from Asbury University," February 16, 2023, emphasis in original.

7. Kevin Brown, "An Update," February 16, 2023; Kevin Brown email, May 11, 2023.

8. Tim Beougher, Facebook post, February 13, 2023.

9. Brandon Porter, "Revival Fires Stir Again at Asbury," *Baptist Press*, February 12, 2023, https://www.baptistpress.com /resource-library/news/revival-fires-stir-again-at-asbury/.

10. Bill Elliff, "Reflections from Asbury (Part 2)," blog, February 13, 2023, https://billelliff.org/blogs/news/reflections-from -asbury-part-2?_pos=6&_sid=47f9e7a91&_ss=r.

11. Steve Seamands, "Asbury Revival," interview with Jimmy Siebert and Drew Steadman, "Passion and Purpose" podcast, February 21, 2023.

12. J. D. Walt email, May 11, 2023.

13. Timothy Tennent interview, March 29, 2023.

14. Laura Levens, "What I Witnessed This Week at the Asbury Revival," *Baptist News Global*, February 16, 2023, https:// baptistnews.com/article/what-i-witnessed-this-week-at-the -asbury-revival/.

15. Sherry Powers interview, April 24, 2023.

16. Kevin Brown, livestream, Avon Park, February 10, 2023; CBN, "The Asbury Awakening."

17. David Swartz interview, March 3, 2023.

18. Glenn Hamilton interview, April 13, 2023.

19. Asbury Seminary Outpouring video, Jason Vickers and James Thobaden, February 16, 2023.

20. Mark Whitworth interview, March 29, 2023; Timothy Tennent, "Thoughts on the Asbury Awakening," February 14, 2023; Liza Evseeva and Jake Traylor, "A Nonstop Kentucky Prayer 'Revival' Is Going Viral on TikTok, and People Are Traveling Thousands of Miles to Take Part" NBC News, February 15, 2023, https://www.nbcnews.com/tech/internet

/asbury-university-revival-college-kentucky-going-viral
-tiktok-rcna70686; Amber Ferguson, "Nonstop Worship
Service at Kentucky College Set to End after Attracting
Thousands," *Washington Post*, February 18, 2023, https://www
.washingtonpost.com/religion/2023/02/18/asbury-university
-revival-kentucky/.

21. Thomas Lyons, "When a Christian Revival Goes Viral," *The
    Atlantic*, February 23, 2023, https://www.theatlantic.com
    /ideas/archive/2023/02/asbury-kentucky-university-christian
    -revival/673176/.

22. Timothy Tennent, "Thoughts."

23. Sherry Powers interview, April 24, 2023.

24. Sherry Powers interview, April 24, 2023.

25. Heather Hornbeak interview, April 28, 2023.

26. Alexandra Presta, "God Cares About the Safety of His People,"
    Asbury Collegian, February 14, 2023.

27. Lena Marlowe, interview with Cameron Bertuzzi, "Capturing
    Christianity," YouTube, February 27, 2023.

28. Kevin Brown, "Update," February 14, 2023.

29. Kevin Brown, "Update," February 16, 2023.

30. Larry Brown interview, April 28, 2023.

31. Lyons, "When a Christian Revival Goes Viral."

32. CBN, "The Asbury Awakening."

33. Harold Rainwater interview, May 1, 2023.

34. Heather Hornbeak, journal, day 12, no. 2, March 15, 2023.

CHAPTER SIX: SHEPHERDING THE UNEXPECTED

1. Jeannie Banter, retired faculty prayer meeting, May 9, 2023.
   A core group consisted of President Brown, Sarah Baldwin,
   Jeannie Banter, Madeline Black, Glenn Hamilton, Greg
   Haseloff, Zach Meerkreebs, David Thomas, and Mark
   Whitworth. David Thomas interview, April 19, 2023; Glenn
   Hamilton interview, April 13, 2023.

2. Glenn Hamilton interview, April 13, 2023; Sherry Powers
   interview, April 24, 2023; Timothy Tennent interview, March
   29, 2023.

3.   Mark Whitworth interview, March 29, 2023.
4.   Sarah Baldwin interview, March 24, 2023; Glenn Hamilton interview, April 13, 2023; Mark Whitworth interview, March 29, 2023.
5.   Sherry Powers interview, April 24, 2023.
6.   Timothy Tennent interview, March 29, 2023.
7.   Paul Dupree interview, April 14, 2023.
8.   Sarah Baldwin Facebook post, February 16, 2023.
9.   Paul Dupree interview, April 14, 2023.
10.   Sarah Baldwin Facebook post, February 25, 2023.
11.   Mark Whitworth interview, March 39, 2023; Sherry Powers interview, April 24, 2023.
12.   Glenn Hamilton interview, April 13, 2023.
13.   Sarah Baldwin interview, March 24, 2023.
14.   Mark Troyer interview, March 8, 2023; Jeannie Banter, retired faculty prayer meeting, May 9, 2023.
15.   Mark Troyer interview, March 8, 2023; Jeannie Banter, retired faculty prayer meeting, May 9, 2023.
16.   Harold Rainwater interview, May 1, 2023.
17.   Glenn Hamilton interview, April 13, 2023; Paul Dupree interview, April 14, 2023.
18.   Sarah Baldwin interview, March 24, 2023; Greg Haseloff interview, April 12, 2023.
19.   Sarah Baldwin interview, March 24, 2023.
20.   Sarah Baldwin interview, March 24, 2023; "Beyond Hughes Auditorium," Light and Life Podcast, March 13, 2023.
21.   Laura Levens, "What I Witnessed This Week at the Asbury Revival," *Baptist News Global,* February 16, 2023, https://baptistnews.com/article/what-i-witnessed-this-week-at-the-asbury-revival/.
22.   Craig Keener, "Opinion: What Is Revival—and Is It Happening at Asbury?" February 16, 2023, https://julieroys.com/opinion-what-revival-happening-asbury/.
23.   Bill Elliff, "Reflections from Asbury (Part 1)," blog, February 11, 2023, https://billelliff.org/blogs/news/reflections-from-asbury.

24. David Swartz interview, March 3, 2023.
25. Walt, *Revival Town* Podcast; Larry Brown interview, April 28, 2023.
26. Lawson Stone, Revival Diary, February 8–24, 2023.
27. Bob Smietana, "Todd Bentley Investigation Finds 'Steady Pattern' of Immoral Conduct," *Christianity Today*, January 3, 2020, https://www.christianitytoday.com/news/2020/january /todd-bentley-charismatic-preacher-investigation-miscon- duct.html.
28. Mark Whitworth interview, March 29, 2023.
29. Rick Pidcock, "Pastor Greg Locke Is All Over the Internet Spreading Conspiracies; Here's Why You Shouldn't Believe Him," *Baptist News Global*, August 2, 2021, https://baptistnews .com/article/pastor-greg-locke-is-all-over-the-internet -spreading-conspiracies-heres-why-you-shouldnt-believe -him/; Mark Whitworth interview, March 29, 2023.
30. Thomas Lyons, "When a Christian Revival Goes Viral," *The Atlantic*, February 23, 2023, https://www.theatlantic.com/ideas /archive/2023/02/asbury-kentucky-university-christian-revival /673176/; Molly Olmstead, "Why Christian Nationalists Are into 'Jumbo-Sized' Shofars," *Slate*, September 23, 2022, https://slate.com/news-and-politics/2022/09/oversize-shofars -christian-nationalists-trump.html.
31. Larry Brown interview, April 28, 2023; Mark Whitworth interview, March 29, 2023.

CHAPTER SEVEN: SECURITY AND SAFETY

1. Laura Levens, "What I Witnessed This Week at the Asbury Revival," *Baptist News Global*, February 16, 2023, https:// baptistnews.com/article/what-i-witnessed-this-week-at-the -asbury-revival/.
2. Deborah Laker, "Two Asbury Students Reflect on What the Revival Means for Gen Z's Faith," *Religion Unplugged*, February 22, 2023, religionunplugged.com.
3. David Hay interview, April 25, 2023.

4. Sherry Powers interview, April 24, 2023.

5. Larry Brown interview, April 28, 2023; conversation with anonymous worship leader, Spring 2023.

6. Glen Hamilton interview, April 13, 2023; David Hay interview, April 25, 2023.

7. David Hay interview, April 25, 2023.

8. Heather Hornbeak interview, April 28, 2023.

9. David Hay interview, April 25, 2023.

10. David Hay interview, April 25, 2023; Glenn Hamilton interview, April 13, 2023; Paul Dupree interview, April 14, 2023.

11. David Hay interview, April 14, 2023.

12. Timothy Tennent interview, March 29, 2023; Paul Dupree interview, April 14, 2023; Glenn Hamilton interview, April 13, 2023.

13. Greg Haseloff interview, April 5, 2023.

14. Timothy Tennent interview, March 29, 2023.

15. Mark Whitworth interview, March 29, 2023.

16. Glenn Hamilton interview, April 13, 2023.

17. Craig Keener, "People Met Jesus Deeply Here: Craig Keener on the Asbury Outpouring," *The Pneuma Review*, March 13, 2023, http://pneumareview.com/people-met-jesus-deeply-here-craig-keener-on-the-asbury-outpouring/.

18. Paul Dupree interview, April 14, 2023; Mark Whitworth interview, March 24, 2023; Timothy Tennent interview, March 29, 2023.

19. Mark Whitworth interview, March 29, 2023; Timothy Tennent, "Thoughts on the Asbury Awakening," February 14, 2023.

20. Paul Dupree interview, April 14, 2023.

21. Lawson Stone, Revival Diary, February 8–24, 2023.

22. David Hay interview, April 25, 2023.

23. Harold Rainwater interview, May 1, 2023.

24. David Hay interview, April 25, 2023; Glenn Hamilton interview, April 13, 2023.

25. Harold Rainwater interview, May 1, 2023.

26. Harold Rainwater interview, May 1, 2023.

27. David Hay interview, April 13, 2023.

28. Glenn Hamilton interview, April 13, 2023.
29. Stone, Revival Diary.

CHAPTER EIGHT: VOLUNTEERS

1. Daniel Silliman, "'No Celebrities Except Jesus': How Asbury Protected the Revival," *Christianity Today*, February 23, 2023, https://www.christianitytoday.com/news/2023/february/asbury -revival-outpouring-protect-work-admin-volunteers.html.
2. Mark Troyer interview, March 8, 2023.
3. Mark Whitworth interview, March 29, 2023; Mark Troyer interview, March 8, 2023; Glenn Hamilton interview, April 13, 2023; https://lofthousecollective.com.
4. Brad Atkinson interview, April 20, 2023; Doug Butler, retired faculty prayer meeting, March 14, 2023.
5. Sarah Baldwin Facebook post, February 16, 2023.
6. Heather Hornbeak, journal, day 14, no. 4, February 21, 2023.
7. Mark Swayze interview, April 18, 2023; Timothy Tennent interview, March 29, 2023.
8. Bud Simon, Wilmore Missions Network meeting, April 12, 2023.
9. David Thomas interview, April 19, 2023.
10. Bud Simon, Wilmore Missions Network meeting, April 12, 2023; "L. P." anonymous interview, April 20, 2023.
11. Sarah Baldwin Facebook post, February 16, 2023.
12. Madeline Black interview, April 21, 2023; "L. P." anonymous interview, April 20, 2023.
13. Madeline Black email, April 20, 2023.
14. Madeline Black interview, April 21, 2023; David Thomas interview, April 19, 2023; Mark Swayze interview, April 18, 2023.
15. Mark Troyer interview, March 8, 2023 (200); Mark Swayze interview, April 18, 2023 (250 to 300).
16. Madeline Black interview, April 21, 2023.
17. "L. P." anonymous interview, April 20, 2023; Mark Swayze interview, April 18, 2023.
18. David Thomas interview, April 19, 2023; Amber Ferguson, "Nonstop Worship Service at Kentucky College Set to End

after Attracting Thousands," *Washington Post*, February 18, 2023, https://www.washingtonpost.com/religion/2023/02/18 /asbury-university-revival-kentucky/.

19. Mark Swayze Facebook post, February 16, 2023.

20. Mark Swayze interview, April 18, 2023; Madeline Black interview, April 21, 2023; Craig Keener, "Opinion: What Is Revival—and Is It Happening at Asbury?" February 16, 2023, https://baptistnews.com/article/what-i-witnessed-this-week -at-the-asbury-revival/.

21. "L. P." anonymous interview, April 20, 2023.

22. "L. P." anonymous interview, April 20, 2023.

23. Glenn Hamilton interview, April 13, 2023; Mark Swayze interview, April 18, 2023; Mark Whitworth interview, March 29, 2023; Craig Keener, "People Met Jesus Deeply Here: Craig Keener on the Asbury Outpouring," *The Pneuma Review*, March 13, 2023, http://pneumareview.com/people-met-jesus -deeply-here-craig-keener-on-the-asbury-outpouring/.

24. Glenn Hamilton interview, April 13, 2023.

25. Silliman, "'No Celebrities Except Jesus.'"

26. Sarah Baldwin Facebook post, February 16, 2023.

27. Mark Troyer interview, Mark 8, 2023.

28. Mark Troyer interview, March 8, 2023; Jonathan Raymond conversation, May 8, 2023.

29. Glenn Hamilton interview, April 13, 2023.

30. Sherry Powers interview, April 24, 2023.

31. Kevin Brown email, May 11, 2023; Glenn Hamilton interview, April 13, 2023.

32. Laura Levens, "What I Witnessed This Week at the Asbury Revival," *Baptist News Global*, February 16, 2023, https:// baptistnews.com/article/what-i-witnessed-this-week-at-the -asbury-revival/.

33. Jeannette Davis, retired faculty prayer meeting, March 14, 2023.

34. Glenn Hamilton interview, April 13, 2023; David Thomas interview, April 19, 2023; Jeannette Davis, retired faculty prayer meeting, March 14, 2023.

35. Darlene Elliott conversation, April 11, 2023; Bonnie Lashbrook, retired faculty prayer meeting, March 14, 2023.
36. Mark Whitworth interview, March 29, 2023.
37. Mark Troyer interview, March 8, 2023.
38. Timothy Tennent interview, March 29, 2023.
39. Silliman, "'No Celebrities Except Jesus.'"
40. Suzanne Nicholson, "When Streams of Living Water Become a Flood: Revival at Asbury University," *Firebrand Magazine*, February 21, 2023, https://firebrandmag.com/articles/when-streams-of-living-water-become-a-flood-revival-at-asbury-university.
41. Keith Madill conversation, February 21, 2023.
42. Daryl Diddle, "A Little Update Here Regarding the Events at Asbury University," email, February 17, 2023.
43. Jonathan Raymond conversation, May 8, 2023.
44. Sarah Baldwin Facebook post, February 16, 2023.

CHAPTER NINE: MEDIA COVERAGE

1. Robert E. Coleman, ed., *One Divine Moment; The Account of the Asbury Revival of 1970*, Anniversary Edition (1970; repr., Wilmore, KY: First Fruits Press, 2013), 69–81.
2. Mark Whitworth interview, March 29, 2023; "Tucker Carlson Highlights the Asbury Revival (2/12/23)," YouTube; Liza Evseeva and Jake Traylor, "A Nonstop Kentucky Prayer 'Revival' Is Going Viral on TikTok, and People Are Traveling Thousands of Miles to Take Part," NBC News, February 15, 2023, https://www.nbcnews.com/tech/internet/asbury-university-revival-college-kentucky-going-viral-tiktok-rcna70686; A. J. Willingham, "A Nonstop Worship Gathering at a Kentucky School Echoes an Old Christian Tradition," CNN, February 18, 2023, https://www.cnn.com/2023/02/18/us/asbury-revival-christian-what-is-cec/index.html.
3. Mark Whitworth interview, March 29, 2023.
4. Mark Whitworth interview, March 29, 2023.
5. [Jonny Williams], "A New Awakening; A Christian College in Kentucky Has Experienced a Religious Awakening," *The*

Economist, March 3, 2023; Thomas Lyons, "When a Christian Revival Goes Viral," *The Atlantic*, February 23, 2023, https://www.theatlantic.com/ideas/archive/2023/02/asbury-kentucky-university-christian-revival/673176/; Daniel Silliman, "'No Celebrities Except Jesus': How Asbury Protected the Revival," *Christianity Today*, February 23, 2023, https://www.christianitytoday.com/news/2023/february/asbury-revival-outpouring-protect-work-admin-volunteers.html. Ruth Graham, "Woodstock for Christians: Revival Draws Thousands to Kentucky Town," *New York Times*, February 20, 2023, https://www.nytimes.com/2023/02/23/us/kentucky-revival-asbury-university.html; Amber Ferguson, "Nonstop Worship Service at Kentucky College Set to End after Attracting Thousands," *Washington Post*, February 18, 2023, https://www.washingtonpost.com/religion/2023/02/18/asbury-university-revival-kentucky/; Aaron Griffith, "What Asbury's Christian Revival Says about America's Need for Connections," *Time Magazine*, February 28, 2023, https://time.com/6258703/asbury-christian-revival-america-connection/; Lee Weeks, "Revival Breaks Out at Asbury University," *Decision Magazine*, February 14, 2023, https://decisionmagazine.com/revival-breaks-out-at-asbury-university/.

6. Paul Dupree interview, April 14, 2023.

7. Robert Danielson conversation, March 1, 2023.

8. Nathan Vick emails, May 4 and 19, 2023.

9. Silliman, "'No Celebrities Except Jesus.'"

10. Many thanks to Nathan Vick, Asbury University Digital Content Manager, Strategic Communications, for providing social media statistics. Emails to author, May 4 and 19, 2023.

11. Heather Hornbeak, journal, day 13, no. 4, April 4, 2023.

12. Heather Hornbeak, journal, day 12, no. 2, March 15, 2023.

13. Heather Hornbeak, journal, day 13, no. 2, April 3, 2023. Howard Dayton is the former CEO of Crown Financial Ministries and Compass-Finances God's Way and author of *Business God's Way*.

14. Heather Hornbeak, journal, day 12, no. 2, March 15, 2023.

15. Heather Hornbeak, journal, day 13, no. 3, April 3, 2023.
16. Heather Hornbeak, journal, day 12, no. 2, March 15, 2023, and email, May 9, 2023. Countries outside the US with the largest number of citizens using social media to follow the course of the revival were Brazil (20,054), Canada (20,034), United Kingdom (11,383), Australia (5,705), India (4,443), Mexico (4,309), Germany (4,233), France (3,053), and the Netherlands (2,983).

CHAPTER TEN: WILMORE

1. Harold Rainwater interview, May 1, 2023.
2. Ben Witherington, "The Asbury Revival Rolls On," February 17, 2023, https://www.patheos.com/blogs/bibleandculture/2023/02/17/the-asbury-revival-rolls-on/.
3. Lawson Stone, Revival Diary, February 8–24, 2023
4. Heather Hornbeak, journal, day 13, no. 4, April 4, 2023.
5. Steve Rehner, email to friends, February 20, 2023.
6. Harold Rainwater interview, May 1, 2023.
7. Steve Rehner, email to friends, February 20, 2023.
8. Paul Stephens email, April 5, 2023; Emily Allen email, May 16, 2023; Greg Haseloff interview, April 5, 2023; Pete Greig, YouTube, February 8, 2023; Deborah Laker, "Two Asbury Students Reflect on What the Revival Means for Gen Z's Faith," *Religion Unplugged*, February 22, 2023, https://religionunplugged.com/news/2023/2/22/what-the-asbury-revival-means-for-gen-zs-faith; Glenn Hamilton interview, April 13, 2023; [Jonny Williams], "A New Awakening; A Christian College in Kentucky Has Experienced a Religious Awakening," *The Economist*, March 3, 2023; Timothy Tennent, "Spiritual Awakening at Asbury," *Alumni Link*, April 4, 2023, https://asburyseminary.edu/elink/dr-timothy-tennent-spiritual-awakening-at-asbury/. The following are the varying estimates for the number of Wilmore residents and visitors, February 8–23, 2023: 50,000—Asbury eNews, May 3, 2023, and Glenn Hamilton interview; "Over 50,000"—Kevin Brown; "Up to 70,000"—Asbury spokesperson quoted in "A

New Awakening," *The Economist*; "50,000–70,000"—Timothy Tennent, May 4, 2023; 70,000—Greg Haseloff interview; 100,000—Pete Greig. University and seminary employees working on the Wilmore campuses total 943 and 220 respectively. One would need to add whatever unknown portion commute into Wilmore for a grand total of the village's overload in February 2023.

9. Timothy Tennent interview, March 29, 2023.

10. Jessica LaGrone email, April 21, 2023; Nathan Elliott email, May 9, 2023; D. Merricks email, May 9, 2023.

11. Timothy Tennent interview, March 29, 2023;

12. Timothy Tennent interview, March 29, 2023; Gregg A. Okesson, "Asbury Provost Reflects on Revival," Association of Theological Schools, *Colloquy Online*, March 2023, https://www.ats.edu/files/galleries/asbury-provost-reflects-on-revival.pdf.

13. David Thomas interview, April 19, 2023; Timothy Tennent interview, May 29, 2023.

14. Paul Dupree interview, April 14, 2023.

15. Keith Madill conversation, February 21, 2023; Paul Dupree interview, April 14, 2023; Brad Atkinson interview, April 20, 2023; Jerry Coleman, Notes from Jerry, February 22, 2023; Steve Rehner email to friends, February 20, 2023.

16. Daryl Diddle, "A Little Update," February 17, 2023.

17. Keith Madill conversation, February 21, 2023.

18. Ben Witherington, "The Asbury Revival Rolls On"; Paul Dupree interview, April 14, 2023; Yale Kim, "Eyewitness Report: A Spiritual Revival Is Breaking Out at Asbury University in Kentucky—Could It Spread Across the Country and World?" February 16, 2023, https://allisrael.com/eyewitness-report-a-spiritual-revival-is-breaking-out-at-asbury-university-in-kentucky-could-it-spread-across-the-country-and-world.

19. Randy Rainwater, "Asbury Revival, Refugees, New Hope, My Parking Spot, and Leonard Fitch," Well Versed World, Facebook post.

20. Rainwater, "Asbury Revival."

CHAPTER ELEVEN: SPREADING NEAR AND FAR

1. Kevin Brown, email to Asbury constituents, February 16, 2023.
2. Suzanne Nicholson, "When Streams of Living Water Become a Flood: Revival at Asbury University," *Firebrand Magazine,* February 21, 2023, https://firebrandmag.com/articles/when -streams-of-living-water-become-a-flood-revival-at-asbury -university.
3. Brandon Porter, "Revival Fires Stir Again at Asbury," *Baptist Press,* February 12, 2023, https://www.baptistpress.com/resource -library/news/revival-fires-stir-again-at-asbury/.
4. Sarah Baldwin Facebook posts, February 17 and 25, 2023.
5. David Thomas interview, April 19, 2023.
6. Sherry Powers interview, April 24, 2023.
7. Andy Miller III, *More to the Story* podcast, February 20, 2023.
8. Daryl Diddle, "A Little Update," February 17, 2023.
9. Craig Keener, "People Met Jesus Deeply Here: Craig Keener on the Asbury Outpouring," *The Pneuma Review,* March 13, 2023, http://pneumareview.com/people-met-jesus-deeply-here -craig-keener-on-the-asbury-outpouring/.
10. Timothy Tennent interview, March 29, 2023.
11. Timothy Tennent interview, March 29, 2023.
12. Mark Troyer interview, March 8, 2023.
13. Sarah Baldwin Facebook post, February 25, 2023.
14. Mark Whitworth interview, March 29, 2023.
15. Greg Haseloff, Wilmore Missions Network meeting, April 12, 2023.
16. Sarah Baldwin Facebook post, February 17, 2023.
17. Austin Schick, "Days Long 'Revival' Attracts Thousands to Asbury University," Spectrum News, February 16, 2023, https://spectrumnews1.com/ky/louisville/news/2023/02/16 /asbury-university-revival.
18. Amber Ferguson, "Nonstop Worship Service at Kentucky College Set to End after Attracting Thousands," *Washington Post,* February 18, 2023, https://www.washingtonpost.com /religion/2023/02/18/asbury-university-revival-kentucky/.

19. Lisa Evseeva and Jake Traylor, "A Nonstop Kentucky Prayer 'Revival' Is Going Viral on TikTok, and People Are Traveling Thousands of Miles to Take Part," NBC News, February 15, 2023, https://www.nbcnews.com/tech/internet/asbury -university-revival-college-kentucky-going-viral-tiktok -rcna70686.

20. Evseeva and Traylor, "A Nonstop Kentucky Prayer 'Revival' Is Going Viral on TikTok."

21. Ferguson, "Nonstop Worship."

22. Jeannie Banter, retired faculty prayer meeting, May 9, 2023; Sarah Baldwin Facebook post, February 25, 2023.

23. Jeannie Banter, retired faculty prayer meeting, May 9, 2005.

24. Mark Troyer interview, March 8, 2023.

25. Bill Elliff, "Reflections from Asbury (Part 1)," blog, February 11, 2023, https://billelliff.org/blogs/news/reflections-from-asbury.

26. Max Vanderpool, "The Revival Known Around the World," *Jessamine County Living*, Spring 2023.

27. Vanderpool, "The Revival."

28. Kevin Brown, "Update," February 24, 2023.

29. Robert Kanary, "The Long but Little-Known History," blog, February 27, 2023, https://salvomag.com/post/asbury -university-revivals.

30. Stevan Sheets, Facebook, February 14, 2023.

31. Porter, "Revival Fires."

32. Gregg A. Okesson, "Asbury Provost Reflects on Revival," Association of Theological Schools, *Colloquy Online*, March 2023, https://www.ats.edu/files/galleries/asbury-provost-reflects -on-revival.pdf; Brad Atkinson drew the same transfiguration analogy, April 20, 2023.

33. Pete Greig, YouTube, February 8, 2023.

34. Steve Seamands, Thoughtful Fellowship Book Club meeting, April 5, 2023.

35. Gina Christian, "'Jesus Was Right Next to Me': Asbury Revival Sets Catholics on Fire with Holy Spirit," *Detroit Catholic*, February 17, 2023, https://www.detroitcatholic.com/news

/jesus-was-right-next-to-me-asbury-revival-sets-catholics-on
-fire-with-holy-spirit.

36. Diane Troyer email, March 8, 2023; Sarah Baldwin interview, March 24, 2023; Kanary, "The Long but Little-Known History," blog, February 27, 2023.

37. Diane Troyer email, March 8, 2023;

38. Alexandra Presta, "Learning to Love: A Sunday Night Revival Update," *Asbury Collegian*, February 12, 2023, http://www.theasburycollegian.com/2023/02/learning-to-love-a-sunday-night-revival-update/.

39. Rob Lim interview, May 2, 2023.

CHAPTER TWELVE: CONCLUSION OR COMMENCEMENT

1. Robert Kanary, *Spontaneous Revivals: Asbury College 1905–2006: Firsthand Accounts of Lives Transformed* (Lexington, KY: CreateSpace, 2017), i.

2. Rich Manieri, "Leave the Labels to History and Watch God Work," *Asbury Collegian*, February 24, 2023, https://www.theasburycollegian.com/2023/02/leave-the-labels-to-history-and-watch-god-work/.

3. Kanary, *Spontaneous Revivals*, 77–79.

4. Anna Lowe, "When the Dust Settles," *Asbury Collegian*, February 15, 2023, http://www.theasburycollegian.com/2023/02/when-the-dust-settles/.

5. Timothy Tennent, "Thoughts on the Asbury Awakening," February 14, 2023, https://timothytennent.com/thoughts-on-the-asbury-awakening/.

6. Joseph Thacker, *Asbury College: Vision and Miracle* (Nappanee, IN: Evangel Press, 1990), 198–201; Edward McKinley and Jonathan Kulaga, eds., *A Purpose Rare: 125 Years of Asbury University* (Wilmore, KY: Asbury University, 2015), 123; Henry C. James et al., *Halls Aflame: An Account of the Spontaneous Revivals at Asbury College in 1950 and 1958* (Wilmore, KY: First Fruits Press, 2013); Robert E. Coleman, ed., *One Divine Moment: The Account of the Asbury Revival of*

1970, Anniversary Edition (1970; repr., Wilmore, KY: First Fruits Press, 2013).

7. John Wesley Hughes, *Autobiography of John Wesley Hughes* (Louisville, KY: Pentecostal Publishing Company, 1923), 126; Thacker, *Asbury College,* 49.

8. Kevin Brown, "The Difficulty of Being True to Yourself," Asbury University chapel, February 3, 2023, https://www.asbury.edu/podcasts/108300/.

APPENDIX A

1. Helen Jin Kim, "What's So Special about the Asbury Revivals?" February 23, 2023; https://divinity.uchicago.edu/sightings/articles/whats-so-special-about-asbury-revivals.

2. Mark Troyer interview, March 8, 2023; Duncan Edward Pile, "Politicizing the Asbury Revival," Patheos blog, February 20, 2023, https://www.patheos.com/blogs/duncanedwardpile/2023/02/politicising-the-asbury-revival/.

3. "F. G." anonymous conversation, February 21, 2023.

4. "N. B." anonymous conversation, March 19, 2023.

5. Kelly Bixler email, April 11, 2023; Kevin Brown email, May 11, 2023.

6. Amber Ferguson, "Nonstop Worship Service at Kentucky College Set to End after Attracting Thousands," *Washington Post,* February 18, 2023, https://www.washingtonpost.com/religion/2023/02/18/asbury-university-revival-kentucky/.

7. Thomas Lyons, "When Christian Revival Goes Viral," *The Atlantic,* February 23, 2023, https://www.theatlantic.com/ideas/archive/2023/02/asbury-kentucky-university-christian-revival/673176/.

8. Ben Witherington, "The Asbury Revival Rolls On," February 17, 2023, https://www.patheos.com/blogs/bibleandculture/2023/02/17/the-asbury-revival-rolls-on/.

9. Craig Keener, unpublished journal, emailed to author, April 15, 2023.

10. Joseph Thacker, *Asbury College: Vision and Miracle* (Nappanee, IN: Evangel Press, 1990), 198–201; Kanary, *Spontaneous*

Revivals; McKinley, *Purpose Rare*, 123; James, *Halls Aflame*; Coleman, *One Divine Moment*.

11. Craig Keener, "People Met Jesus Deeply Here: Craig Keener on the Asbury Outpouring," *The Pneuma Review*, March 13, 2023, http://pneumareview.com/people-met-jesus-deeply-here -craig-keener-on-the-asbury-outpouring/.

12. Keener, "People Met Jesus Deeply Here."

13. Keener, "People Met Jesus Deeply Here."

14. "President's Updates," April 23, 2023.

15. Chip Hutcheson, "Revival Spreading to Other Colleges and Universities," *Kentucky Today*, February 14, 2023, https://www .kentuckytoday.com/baptist_life/revival-spreading-to-other -colleges-and-universities/article_3d8c4e14-acab-11ed-a867 -af396e32f340.html.

16. Brandon Porter, "Revival Fires Stir Again at Asbury," *Baptist Press*, February 12, 2023, https://www.baptistpress.com /resource-library/news/revival-fires-stir-again-at-asbury/.

17. Greg Haseloff, Wilmore Missions Network meeting, April 12, 2023; David Thomas interview, April 12, 2023.

18. Lawson Stone, Revival Diary, February 8–24, 2023.

19. Thomas Lyons, "Asbury Revival: Answers to Help Us Understand What God Might Be Up To," Seminary Now Blogpost, February 14, 2023, https://seminarynow.com/pages /blog?p=asbury-revival-answers-to-help-us-understand.

20. Jon Brown, "Christian University in Kentucky Draws Pilgrims Nationwide Amid Spiritual Revival: 'Gives Me So Much Hope,'" Fox News, February 15, 2023, https://www.foxnews .com/us/christian-university-kentucky-draws-pilgrims -nationwide-spiritual-revival-gives-me-so-much-hope.

21. Alexandra Presta, "Learning to Love: A Sunday Night Revival Update," *Asbury Collegian*, February 12, 2023, http://www .theasburycollegian.com/2023/02/learning-to-love-a-sunday -night-revival-update/.

22. Alexandra Presta, "Learning to Love."

23. Daniel Silliman, "'No Celebrities Except Jesus': How Asbury Protected the Revival," *Christianity Today*, February 23, 2023,

https://www.christianitytoday.com/news/2023/february
/asbury-revival-outpouring-protect-work-admin-volunteers
.html.

24. Harold Rainwater interview, May 1, 2023.

25. Ben Witherington blog, February 17, 2023, https://www
.patheos.com/blogs/bibleandculture/2023/02/17/the-asbury
-revival-rolls-on/.

26. Rob Lim interview, May 2, 2023.

27. Eugene Peterson, *A Long Obedience in the Same Direction*
(Downers Grove, IL: InterVarsity Press, 1980).

28. Timothy Tennent, "Spiritual Awakening at Asbury"; Stephen
A. Seamands, "What Happens in Revival?" *Good News
Magazine*, February 13, 2023, https://goodnewsmag.org/what
-happens-in-revival/; Jonathan Edwards quoted in Seamands,
"What Happens in Revival?"

29. Suzanne Nicholson, "When Streams of Living Water Become
a Flood: Revival at Asbury University," *Firebrand Magazine*,
February 21, 2023, https://firebrandmag.com/articles/when
-streams-of-living-water-become-a-flood-revival-at-asbury
-university.

30. Greg Haseloff interview, April 5, 2023; Madeline Black interview, April 21, 2023.

31. "In Depth," Mark Irons Report, EWTN Global Catholic
Network.

32. Greg Haseloff interview, April 5, 2023.

33. Craig Keener, "People Met Jesus."

34. Madeline Black interview, April 21, 2023; Rob Lim interview,
May 2, 2023.

35. Mark Swayze interview, April 18, 2023.

36. "L. P." anonymous interview, April 20, 2023; Mark Swayze
interview, April 18, 2023; Madeline Black interview, April
21, 2023.

37. James Thobaden, "Reflection on the Outpouring," Asbury
Seminary Outpouring video, February 16, 2023.

38. Rob Lim interview, May 2, 2023; Steve Seamands, Thoughtful
Fellowship Book Club, April 5, 2023.

39. Andy Miller III, "Revival at Asbury—Diane Ury and Charity Johnson," *More to the Story* podcast, February 20, 2023.
40. Rob Lim interview, May 2, 2023.
41. Deborah Laker, "Two Asbury Students Reflect on What the Revival Means for Gen Z's Faith," *Religion Unplugged*, February 22, 2023, https://religionunplugged.com/news/2023/2/22/what-the-asbury-revival-means-for-gen-zs-faith.
42. Mark R. Elliott, *Pieces of History: The Stories behind the Street Names of Wilmore, Kentucky* (Wilmore, KY: City of Wilmore, 2021), 1–2.
43. Glenn Hamilton interview, April 13, 2023.
44. Ferguson, "Nonstop."
45. Ferguson, "Nonstop."
46. Greg Haseloff interview, April 5, 2023.
47. Sarah Baldwin Facebook post, February 25, 2023.
48. Bud Simon, Wilmore Missions Network, April 12, 2023.
49. Sarah Baldwin Facebook post, February 25, 2023.
50. "L. P." anonymous interview, April 20, 2023.
51. E. Stanley Jones, *Christ of the Indian Road* (1925; repr., New York: Abingdon Press, 2014).
52. Frederick Douglass, *Narrative of the Life of Frederick Douglass* (Boston: Anti-Slavery Office, 1845). See also David W. Blight, *Frederick Douglass* (New York: Simon & Schuster, 2018), 58.
53. Aaron Griffith, "What Asbury's Christian Revival Says about America's Need for Connection," *Time Magazine*, February 28, 2023, https://time.com/6258703/asbury-christian-revival-america-connection/; David Swartz, "Sat Tal 1958; Cold War and Caste," Chapter 3, *Facing West: American Evangelicals in an Age of World Christianity* (New York: Oxford University Press, 2020), 65–95.
54. Timothy L. Smith, *Revivalism and Social Reform: American Protestantism on the Eve of the Civil War* (Baltimore: Johns Hopkins University Press, 1957).
55. Craig Keener email, February 26, 2023.
56. Lawson Stone, Revival Diary, February 8–24, 2023.
57. Beougher, Facebook post, February 13, 2023.

58. Greg Haseloff, Wilmore Missions Network, April 12, 2023.

59. Craig Keener, "The Outpouring at Asbury University: Responding to a Critic," Bible Background blog, February 19, 2023, https://craigkeener.com/the-outpouring-at-asbury-university-responding-to-a-critic/.

60. Keener, "The Outpouring."

61. Keener, "The Outpouring."

62. Keener, unpublished journal.

63. Lawson Stone, Revival Diary.

64. Beougher, Facebook post, February 13, 2023.

65. Kevin Brown, "An Update from Asbury University," February 14, 2023; "An Update from Asbury University," February 16, 2023; Statement from Asbury President Dr. Kevin Brown, February 24, 2023; Timothy Tennent, "Thoughts on the Asbury Awakening," February 14, 2023.

66. Kevin Brown email, May 11, 2023; Kevin Brown email, video transcript, May 12, 2023.

about the author

Mark R. Elliott (PhD in modern European and Russian history) has taught at Asbury University (KY); Wheaton College (IL); Samford University (AL); and Southern Wesleyan University (SC). In addition to teaching, Dr. Elliott held administrative posts for nineteen years as director of the Institute for East-West Christian Studies (Wheaton College) and as director of the Global Center (Beeson Divinity School, Samford University).

He is the author of numerous books including *Pawns of Yalta: Soviet Refugees and America's Role in Their Repatriation* and *The Arduous Path of Post-Soviet Protestant Theological Education*. He also is editor emeritus of the *East-West Church and Ministry Report* (www.eastwestreport.org), which he edited for twenty-five years. Dr. Elliott and his wife, Darlene, are the parents of four adult children adopted from Vietnam and Colombia and four grandchildren.

Printed in the USA
CPSIA information can be obtained
at www.ICGtesting.com
LVHW011525300823
755823LV00004B/4